LIST OF TITLES

Already published

A Biochemical Approach to Nutrition	R.A. Freedland, S. Briggs
Biochemical Genetics (second edition)	R.A. Woods
Biological Energy Conservation (second edition)	C.W. Jones
Biomechanics	R.McN. Alexander
Brain Biochemistry (second edition)	H.S. Bachelard
Cellular Degradative Processes	R.T. Dean
Cellular Development	D.R. Garrod
Cellular Recognition	M.F. Greaves
Control of Enzyme Activity	P. Cohen
Cytogenetics of Man and other Animals	A. McDermott
Differentiation of Cells	M. Bownes
Enzyme Kinetics	P.C. Engel
Functions of Biological Membranes	M. Davies
Genetic Engineering: Cloning DNA	D. Glover
Hormone Action	A. Malkinson
Human Evolution	B.A. Wood
Human Genetics	J.H. Edwards
Immunochemistry	M.W. Steward
Insect Biochemistry	H.H. Rees
Isoenzymes	C.C. Rider, C.B. Taylor
Metabolic Regulation	R. Denton, C.I. Pogson
Metals in Biochemistry	P.M. Harrison, R. Hoare
Molecular Virology	T.H. Pennington, D.A. Ritchie
Motility of Living Cells	P. Cappuccinelli
Plant Cytogenetics	D.M. Moore
Polysaccharide Shapes	D.A. Rees
Population Genetics	L.M. Cook
Protein Biosynthesis	A.E. Smith
RNA Biosynthesis	R.H. Burdon
The Selectivity of Drugs	A. Albert
Transport Phenomena in Plants	D.A. Baker

In preparation

Bacterial Taxonomy	D. Jones, M. Goodfellow
Biochemical Systematics	J.B. Harborne
The Cell Cycle	S. Shall
Gene Structure and Function	M. Szekely
Invertebrate Nervous Systems	G. Lunt
Membrane Assembly	J. Haslam

Editor's Foreword

The student of biological science in his final years as an undergraduate and his first years as a graduate is expected to gain some familiarity with current research at the frontiers of his discipline. New research work is published in a perplexing diversity of publications and is inevitably concerned with the minutiae of the subject. The sheer number of research journals and papers also causes confusion and difficulties of assimilation. Review articles usually presuppose a background knowledge of the field and are inevitably rather restricted in scope. There is thus a need for short but authoritative introductions to those areas of modern biological research which are either not dealt with in standard introductory textbooks or are not dealt with in sufficient detail to enable the student to go on from them to read scholarly reviews with profit. This series of books is designed to satisfy this need. The authors have been asked to produce a brief outline of their subject assuming that their readers will have read and remembered much of a standard introductory textbook on biology. This outline then sets out to provide by building on this basis, the conceptual framework within which modern research work is progressing and aims to give the reader an indication of the problems, both conceptual and practical, which must be overcome if progress is to be maintained. We hope that students will go on to read the more detailed reviews and articles to which reference is made with a greater insight and understanding of how they fit into the overall scheme of modern research effort and may thus be helped to choose where to make their own contribution to this effort. These books are guidebooks, not textbooks. Modern research pays scant regard for the academic divisions into which biological teaching and introductory textbooks must, to a certain extent, be divided. We have thus concentrated in this series on providing guides to those areas which fall between, or which involve, several different academic disciplines. It is here that the gap between the textbook and the research paper is widest and where the need for guidance is greatest. In so doing we hope to have extended or supplemented but not supplanted main texts, and to have given students assistance in seeing how modern biological research is progressing, while at the same time providing a foundation for self help in the achievement of successful examination results.

General Editors:

W.J. Brammar, Professor of Biochemistry, University of Leicester, UK

M. Edidin, Professor of Biology, Johns Hopkins University, Baltimore, USA

Biological Energy Conservation

Oxidative Phosphorylation

C.W. Jones

Senior Lecturer,
Department of Biochemistry,
University of Leicester

Second edition

Chapman and Hall
London and New York

First published in 1976
Second edition published in 1981 by
Chapman and Hall Ltd
11 New Fetter Lane, London EC4P 4EE
Published in the USA by
Chapman and Hall
in association with Methuen, Inc.
733 Third Avenue, New York, NY 10017

Printed and bound in the
United States of America

ISBN 0 412 23360 6

British Library Cataloguing in Publication Data

Jones, Colin William
Biological energy conservation.—2nd ed.—
(Outline studies in biology).
1. Bioenergetics
I. Title II. Series
574.19′121 QH510 80-41792

ISBN 0-412-23360 6

Contents

Acknowledgements

I am deeply indebted to Bruce Haddock, Alan McKay and Michael Dawson for their careful and critical reading of the manuscript, and to numerous colleagues for their guidance and help on specific points. My sincere thanks are also due to my wife, Beryl, both for her forebearance and encouragement during the writing of this book and for the expert way in which she carried out the secretarial work.

University of Leicester
September 1980 C.W.J.

1 An introduction to bioenergetics

1.1 The flow of energy and materials in biology

The ultimate source of energy to the earth is the electromagnetic radiation of the sun. Higher plants, algae and blue-green bacteria use the visible and near infra-red components of this radiation to drive the reductive assimilation of carbon dioxide (*photoautotrophic growth*) with the concomitant release of molecular oxygen:

$$CO_2 + 2H_2O^* \xrightarrow{\text{light}} [CH_2O] + H_2O + O_2^*.$$

Many species of purple and green bacteria also grow photoautotrophically, but they replace water with other inorganic reductants (e.g. H_2S, $S_2O_3^{2-}$, H_2) and hence do not evolve oxygen:

$$CO_2 + 2H_2S \xrightarrow{\text{light}} [CH_2O] + H_2O + 2S.$$

In addition, some of these bacteria can replace carbon dioxide with partially reduced carbon compounds (e.g. succinate or malate) and thus exhibit *photoheterotrophic growth.* This light-dependent assimilation of carbon by phototrophs is called *photosynthesis*, and the latter is said to be either *oxygenic* or *anoxygenic* depending on whether it evolves oxygen.

The transfer of reducing equivalents from these reduced donors to carbon dioxide and/or various other carbon substrates and metabolites occurs via the reduction of intermediate acceptors, viz. the complex organic molecules $NADP^+$ and NAD^+ (Section 2.1). This multistep, initially membrane-bound process is potentiated at one or more points by light energy (Fig. 1.1a) and hence is called *photosynthetic electron transfer* (although electrons, hydrogen atoms and hydride ions are all involved). The energy is first trapped using light-absorbing pigments (various types of chlorophylls and carotenoids) and is then converted into a biologically useful form of chemical energy, viz. *adenosine* 5′-triphosphate (ATP; Section 1.2). This conversion process occurs as a direct result of electron transfer and is called *photosynthetic phosphorylation.* The ATP thus produced is used to drive a variety of energy-dependent cellular reactions including the NAD(P)H-dependent biosynthesis of cell materials (*anabolism*), solute transport and, in some organisms, motility.

The end-products of oxygenic photosynthesis, viz. cell material and oxygen, are subsequently used to sustain the growth of chemoheterotrophic organisms. The latter first cleave carbohydrates, lipids and

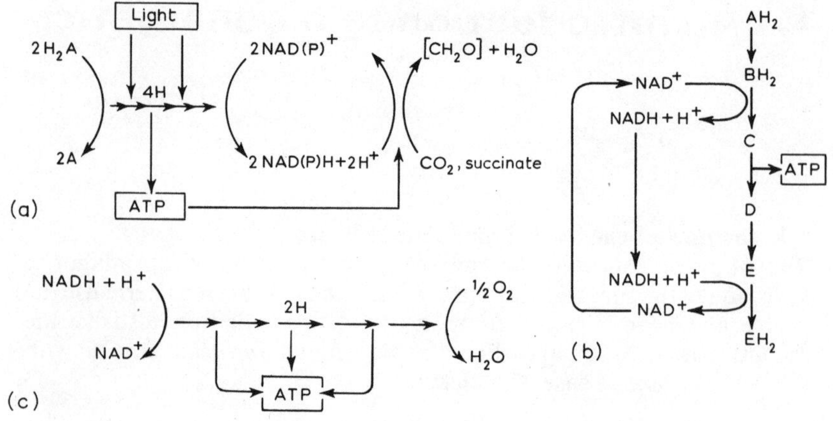

Fig. 1.1 A simplified view of (a) photosynthesis, (b) fermentation, and (c) oxidative phosphorylation.

proteins into their constituent monomers, which are then disproportionated to yield a variety of smaller, more oxidized carbon skeletons plus NAD(P)H. This process (*catabolism*) leads to the release of a small amount of energy which is coupled to ATP synthesis via *substrate-level phosphorylation* (Section 1.4). The latter is a relatively simple, membrane-independent process and is the sole mode of energy conservation available to many fermentative organisms [1]. *Fermentation* is an anaerobic oxidation–reduction process (Fig. 1.1b) in which the exogenous initial reductant and the endogenous terminal oxidant are both organic compounds; NAD(P)H is generated at the expense of the former (or one of its metabolites) and is reoxidized by the latter. Very often a single fermentable substrate such as glucose or an amino acid can give rise to a wide variety of end-products depending on the organism involved (e.g. lactate in animal tissues, ethanol in some yeasts, and lactate, ethanol, butanol, acetone or hydrogen in various species of bacteria); importantly, the average oxidation level of the end-products is equal to that of the initial substrate.

Substrate-level phosphorylation is only a minor phenomenon in aerobic chemoheterotrophs. The latter oxidize NAD(P)H with oxygen, a powerful oxidant, via a complex sequence of membrane-bound oxidation–reduction reactions (*aerobic respiration* or *aerobic electron transfer*); this process releases a large amount of energy which, once again, can be conserved as ATP (*oxidative phosphorylation* or *respiratory chain phosphorylation*) (Fig. 1.1c). A good example of the greater ATP yield from aerobic metabolism compared with anaerobic fermentation is afforded by the oxidation of glucose in animal muscle. Under transiently anaerobic conditions, such as prevail during hard exercise, one mole of glucose is incompletely degraded to two moles of lactate (*glycolysis* or *homolactic fermentation*) with the net production of only two moles of ATP; in contrast, in the presence of oxygen the complete combustion of the glucose to carbon dioxide and water via the combined action of glycolysis, the tricarboxylic acid cycle and respiration yields not less than 36 moles of ATP net. It should be noted that the end-products of aerobic metabolism, viz. carbon dioxide and water, are the major substrates of photosynthesis; respiration and photosynthesis are thus principally responsible for the carbon, hydrogen and oxygen cycles.

A few species of bacteria have improved their capacity for anaerobic energy conservation by carrying out, in addition to substrate-level phosphorylation, a form of respiration which utilizes alternative oxidants to molecular oxygen (*anaerobic respiration*). These include a few highly oxidized organic molecules (e.g. fumarate and carbon dioxide) and, most importantly, certain nitrogen and sulphur compounds; the latter cover a wide range of oxidation states and, in the main, undergo oxidation–reduction in two-electron steps (oxidation states in brackets):

$$NO_3^-(+5) \rightleftharpoons NO_2^-(+3) \begin{array}{l} \nearrow [NO(+2)] \rightarrow N_2O(+1) \rightarrow N_2(O) \rightarrow NH_3(-3) \\ \swarrow [NOH(+1)] \leftarrow NH_2OH(-1) \leftarrow NH_3(-3) \end{array}$$

$$SO_4^{2-}(+6) \rightleftharpoons SO_3^{2-}(+4) \rightleftharpoons S_2O_3^{2-}(+2) \rightleftharpoons S(O) \rightleftharpoons H_2S(-2).$$

The sequential reductions of nitrate to nitrogen, and of sulphate to sulphide, constitute the phenomena of *denitrification* and *desulphurification*, respectively. It should be noted that because of its inert nature N_2 cannot easily be used as an oxidant; indeed, the reduction of nitrogen to ammonia (*nitrogen fixation*) is an energy-dependent reaction. Most of these compounds are relatively weak oxidants compared with oxygen; the ATP yield from anaerobic respiration is, therefore, generally lower than from aerobic respiration, but higher than that usually obtained from anaerobic fermentation.

An even more specialized group of bacteria, the *chemolithotrophs*, can oxidize a variety of inorganic reductants (e.g. hydrogen, certain nitrogen and sulphur compounds, and Fe^{2+}) using mainly oxygen as the oxidant. These reactions yield widely varied amounts of ATP depending on the precise nature of the electron donor. The sequential oxidations of ammonia to nitrate, and of sulphide to sulphate, constitute the phenomena of *nitrification* and *sulphurification*, respectively; in concert with the reduction reactions outlined above, they are responsible for the nitrogen and sulphur cycles. Since the majority of these chemolithotrophic bacteria are autotrophic they have to use a large proportion of their often meagre ATP supply to drive the reductive assimilation of carbon dioxide; the rates at which these organisms grow are often very low, but their unusual use of inorganic reductants enables them to occupy a safe niche in an otherwise strongly competitive environment.

1.2 Adenosine 5′-triphosphate (ATP)

The common feature of the various types of biological energy conservation systems described above is their ability to conserve energy as ATP. The latter was discovered in muscle extracts by Lohman in 1929,

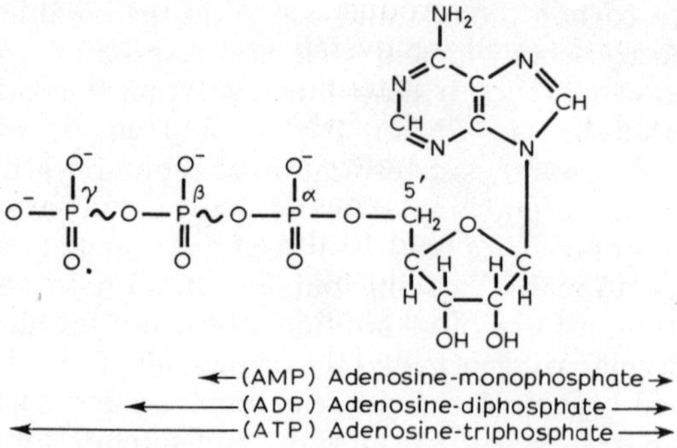

Fig. 1.2 The structure of ATP.

who described its role in glycolysis and later determined its structure (Fig. 1.2). It is composed of a purine base (adenine), a sugar (D-ribofuranose) and three phosphates, the latter being attached to each other via anhydride linkages [2]. At pH 7, three of the four hydroxyl groups in the triphosphate side chain are fully dissociated ($pK_{1-3} \leq 4$) and the fourth is predominantly so ($pK_4 = 6.8$); the molecule thus exhibits close to four negative charges (ATP^{4-}) and under physiological conditions readily binds divalent cations such as Mg^{2+} via the ionized hydroxyl groups on the α and β phosphorus atoms ($Mg.ATP^{2-}$).

Unfortunately, the chemical properties of ATP have often been misunderstood by biochemists. The idea that ATP is a 'high energy' molecule or that it contains a 'high energy phosphate bond' (often denoted by the symbol $\sim$) is incorrect. These misconceptions arise from the fact that when ATP^{4-} undergoes hydrolysis at near neutral pH under the action of an ATPase it produces a proton:

$$ATP^{4-} + H_2O \rightleftharpoons ADP^{3-} + HPO_4^{2-} + H^+. \quad (1.1)$$

(In fact, since the pK_2 of phosphoric acid is 6.8 this reaction produces a mixture of $H_2PO_4^-$ and HPO_4^{2-}, the precise ratio depending on the exact pH; for the sake of simplicity we will assume in this section that the major product is HPO_4^{2-}.) The apparent equilibrium constant (K') of this proton-producing reaction is, therefore, fairly high since the reaction is 'pulled-over' both by the relatively high pH and by the fact that ADP^{3-} and HPO_4^{2-} are both negatively charged resonance hybrids which do not readily recombine. At equilibrium:

$$\Delta G^{\ominus\prime} = -2.303\,RT \log K'$$

where $\Delta G^{\ominus\prime}$ is the standard free energy change (kJ mol^{-1}), R is the gas constant (8.314 J mol^{-1} K^{-1}) and T is the absolute temperature (K). Thus at 298 K (25° C) an observed K' of 3.5×10^5 for ATP hydrolysis is equivalent to a $\Delta G^{\ominus\prime}$ of -31 kJ mol^{-1} ($\equiv -7.4$ kcal mol^{-1}); the minus sign indicates that energy is released from the system. This value, as we shall see below, is only moderately high and is, of course, pH dependent since a proton is one of the products. Most importantly, it reflects the nature of the products and the overall structure of the ATP molecule rather than the chemistry of the terminal anhydride bond itself. This is also true for ADP, the hydrolysis of which to form AMP^{2-} and HPO_4^{2-} is again associated with a moderately high free energy change ($\Delta G^{\ominus\prime} = -31\,\mathrm{kJ\,mol^{-1}}$). The symbol ($\sim$) thus denotes only that hydrolysis of a molecule at that point will lead to the release of a moderate to high amount of free energy. It should be noted, however, that the simple hydrolysis of ATP to ADP and phosphate, with the wasteful release of heat, occurs only rarely *in vivo*, and then only for very good biochemical or physiological reasons.

Since the hydrolysis of ATP is an energy-releasing (*exergonic*) reaction, the synthesis of ATP from ADP and phosphate consumes a similar amount of energy, i.e. the reaction is *endergonic* ($\Delta G^{\ominus\prime} = +31\,\mathrm{kJ\,mol^{-1}}$). The harnessing of the free energy which is released during biological oxidation–reduction reactions to the synthesis of ATP is thus a convenient means of energy conservation, but only in the case of substrate-level phosphorylation is it also a relatively simple process.

The hydrolysis of inorganic pyrophosphate ($P_2O_7^{4-}$; $P \sim P$) to two molecules of phosphate also releases a moderate amount of free energy ($\Delta G^{\ominus\prime} = -22\,\mathrm{kJ\,mol^{-1}}$), and its synthesis is therefore endergonic to the same extent. Interestingly, there is some evidence that pyrophosphate may have preceded ATP as the primary energy carrier in the early stages of evolution, and indeed a few species of photosynthetic bacteria can still synthesize pyrophosphates as an alternative to ATP during photosynthetic phosphorylation.

1.3 Phosphoryl transfer reactions

In contrast to the hydrolysis of ATP^{4-}, ADP^{3-} or pyrophosphate, the hydrolysis of an alcohol phosphate (e.g. AMP^{2-} or glucose-6-phosphate) yields at least one product which is uncharged, and no protons:

$$AMP^{2-} + H_2O \rightleftharpoons \text{adenosine} + HPO_4^{2-} \quad (1.2)$$

$$\text{glucose-6-phosphate}^{2-} + H_2O \rightleftharpoons \text{glucose} + HPO_4^{2-} \quad (1.3)$$

Such hydrolyses are therefore only weakly exergonic ($\Delta G^{\ominus\prime} \leq -17\,\mathrm{kJ\,mol^{-1}}$) and pH-independent. On the other hand, the hydrolyses of relatively unstable phosphoacyl anhydrides (e.g. 1,3-bisphosphoglycerate or acetyl phosphate) and phosphoenol esters (e.g. phosphoenol pyruvate) yield relatively stable, negatively charged products plus a proton:

$$\text{1,3-bisphosphoglycerate}^{4-} + H_2O \rightleftharpoons \text{3-phosphoglycerate}^{3-} + HPO_4^{2-} + H^+ \quad (1.4)$$

$$\text{acetyl phosphate}^{2-} + H_2O \rightleftharpoons \text{acetate}^{-} + HPO_4^{2-} + H^+ \quad (1.5)$$

$$\text{phosphoenol pyruvate}^{2-} + H_2O \rightleftharpoons \text{pyruvate}^{-} + HPO_4^{2-} + H^+. \quad (1.6)$$

Table 1.1 $\Delta G^{\ominus\prime}$ values for the hydrolysis of organic phosphates

Organic phosphate	$\Delta G^{\ominus\prime}$ (kJ mol^{-1})
Phosphoenol pyruvate	−54.5
1,3-bisphosphoglycerate	−49.3
Acetyl phosphate	−43.9
ATP (→ADP + Pi)	−31.0
Glucose-6-phosphate	−13.8
AMP	− 8.4

These reactions are therefore strongly exergonic ($\Delta G^{\ominus\prime} \geq -41$ kJ mol^{-1}) and pH-dependent. It is possible, therefore, to construct a 'league table' of organic phosphates based solely upon their standard free energies of hydrolysis (Table 1.1). In this table, ATP appears about halfway up, below the mixed anhydride phosphates and phosphoenol pyruvate, but above the alcohol phosphates. The biological role of the ATP-ADP system [2] is in accordance with its medium position in the table, viz. to constitute a central phosphoryl ($-PO_3^{2-}$) donor-acceptor system for other organic phosphates. Thus, for example, ATP can donate a phosphoryl group to glucose in the presence of hexokinase, since glucose-6-phosphate is below ATP in the table:

$$ATP^{4-} + \text{glucose} \rightleftharpoons ADP^{3-} + \text{glucose-6-phosphate}^{2-} + H^{+}. \quad (1.7)$$

Conversely, ADP can accept a phosphoryl group from 1,3-bisphosphoglycerate, in the presence of phosphoglycerate kinase, since 1,3-bisphosphoglycerate is above ATP in the table:

$$\text{1,3-bisphosphoglycerate}^{4-} + ADP^{3-} \rightleftharpoons \text{3-phosphoglycerate}^{3-} + ATP^{4-} \quad (1.8)$$

Note that neither of these two reactions proceeds via the hydrolysis of an organic phosphate. However, since thermodynamics is concerned only with the initial and final states of a reaction, and is independent of the true reaction mechanism, the $\Delta G^{\ominus\prime}$ values of these reactions may be determined from the sum of the $\Delta G^{\ominus\prime}$ values of the individual hydro-dehydration reactions. Thus reaction (1.7) may be regarded thermodynamically as the sum of reactions (1.1) and (1.3 in reverse), and reaction (1.8) as the sum of reactions (1.4) and (1.1 in reverse). Both reactions proceed with a slight release of free energy, thus ensuring that their equilibria lie to the right-hand side.

Interestingly, a number of ATP-dependent reactions (e.g. the activation of fatty acids and amino acids) generate inorganic pyrophosphate via the cleavage of ATP between its α and β phosphates; the subsequent hydrolysis of the pyrophosphate by pyrophosphatase ensures that the equilibria of these reactions are displaced in favour of the desired products. A few species of bacteria and protozoa use pyrophosphate instead of ATP as the phosphoryl group donor in specific phosphorylation reactions.

1.4 Substrate-level phosphorylation

Since ATP synthesis can be driven by the transfer of a phosphoryl group from an energy-rich organic phosphate such as 1,3-bisphosphoglycerate, acetyl phosphate or phosphoenol pyruvate, to ADP (Section 1.3), any metabolic sequence which can arrange the generation of these relatively unstable molecules has a potential source of energy which it can harness by substrate-level phosphorylation.

1,3-bisphosphoglycerate arises from the oxidation of 3-phosphoglyceraldehyde during animal and microbial glycolysis:

$$\mathrm{R.\underset{\overset{\|}{O}}{C}H + E.SH + NAD^{+} \rightleftharpoons R.\underset{\overset{\|}{O}}{C} \sim S.E + NADH + H^{+}}$$

$$\mathrm{R.\underset{\overset{\|}{O}}{C} \sim S.E + HPO_4^{2-} \rightleftharpoons R.\underset{\overset{\|}{O}}{C} \sim O.PO_3^{2-} + E.SH}$$

$$\mathrm{R.\underset{\overset{\|}{O}}{C} \sim O.PO_3^{2-} + ADP^{3-} \rightleftharpoons R.\underset{\overset{\|}{O}}{C}.O^{-} + ATP^{4-}.}$$

The initial action of 3-phosphoglyceraldehyde dehydrogenase (E.SH) is to reduce NAD^+. The energy thus released is conserved in the formation of enzyme-bound $-C \sim S-$ ($\Delta G^{\ominus\prime} = -43.1\,\mathrm{kJ\,mol^{-1}}$) and remains conserved following phosphate substitution, to yield 1,3 bisphosphoglycerate; the latter, under the action of phosphoglycerate kinase, finally effects the synthesis of ATP by phosphoryl transfer. Similarly, the oxidation of pyruvate to acetate via acetyl phosphate is an important and frequently encountered pathway of energy conservation during the fermentative growth of many species of anaerobic bacteria. The initial, CoASH-dependent reduction of NAD^+ or ferredoxin (Section 2.3.2) generates CO_2 and acetyl CoA ($C \sim S$; $\Delta G^{\ominus\prime} = -35.0\,\mathrm{kJ\,mol^{-1}}$), which undergoes phosphate substitution to form acetyl phosphate through the action of phosphotransacetylase; the final transfer of a phosphoryl group to ADP is effected by acetate kinase.

The salient features of both these sequential processes are that oxidation–reduction precedes phosphate substitution, which in turn precedes phosphoryl transfer to ADP; the component reactions generate non-phosphorylated and phosphorylated, energy-rich intermediates respectively. It should be noted, however, that substrate-level phosphorylation can also be initiated, albeit fairly rarely, by a lysis reaction rather than an oxidation–reduction reaction, e.g. the formation of acetyl CoA and formate from pyruvate by some bacteria. Substrate-level phosphorylation is therefore characterized by its macroscopic and scalar properties, and by its chemical-coupling mechanism, i.e. the entire sequence of energy transfer is catalysed by essentially soluble enzymes via the stoichiometric formation of covalent, readily detectable (and often easily isolated) intermediates.

1.5 Oxidation–reduction reactions

Oxidation–reduction reactions have been briefly mentioned in the previous section on substrate-level phosphorylation, but they are particularly pertinent to the electron transfer-linked systems of photosynthetic and oxidative phosphorylation. Any oxidation reaction has to be accompanied by a reduction reaction. Thus, during the oxidation of DH_2 to D, A is reduced to AH_2:

$$\begin{array}{ccc} DH_2 & \rightarrow\!\!\supset \;\subset\!\!\leftarrow & A \\ D & \leftarrow\!\!\lrcorner \;\llcorner\!\!\rightarrow & AH_2 \end{array}$$

This four-component system consists of two *redox couples*, D/DH_2 and A/AH_2, each of which can either accept or donate 2H ($\equiv 2H^+ + 2e^-$); other redox couples may transfer hydride ions ($H^- \equiv H^+ + 2e^-$) or simply electrons. If the tendency to donate reducing equivalents is stronger in one couple than the other ($D/DH_2 > A/AH_2$), then there will be a net transfer of reducing equivalents from the more reduced component of the *reducing couple* (DH_2) to the more oxidized component of the *oxidizing couple* (A).

This tendency to donate or accept reducing equivalents can be quantitated by reference to a standard redox couple (i.e. a standard electrode, such as the hydrogen or calomel electrode). When determined under standard conditions of temperature (25°C), concentration ($[DH_2] = [D]$) and pH (7.0 unless stated otherwise) this value is known as the *standard oxidation–reduction (redox) potential* ($E'_{\ominus}$; mV). An equivalent measurement, the *midpoint potential* (E_m), is generally used to express the standard redox potential of membrane-bound redox couples. Since the $E'_{\ominus}$ values of the $NAD^+/NADH + H^+$ and $\frac{1}{2}O_2/H_2O$ couples are − 320 and + 820 mV respectively, then during respiration there is a net transfer of 2H from $NADH(+H^+)$ to oxygen, rather than from water to NAD^+, i.e. in the direction of increasingly positive redox potential.

The $\Delta G^{\ominus\prime}$ of this reaction is related to the difference in the standard redox potential of the oxidizing and reducing couples ($\Delta E'_{\ominus} \equiv E'_{\ominus\,ox} - E'_{\ominus\,red}$) by the simple equation:

$$\Delta G^{\ominus\prime} = -nF\cdot\Delta E'_{\ominus}$$

where n is the number of electrons transferred (2) and F is the Faraday constant ($96.6\,kJ^{-1}\cdot V^{-1}\cdot eq^{-1}$). In order to bring about the reverse reaction, energy would have to be supplied to the system since $\Delta G^{\ominus\prime}$ is now positive (Section 4.6). Good examples of this latter situation are afforded by many phototrophic and chemolithotrophic organisms which, in order to assimilate carbon dioxide, must transfer reducing equivalents from high redox potential donors (e.g. H_2O, H_2S, $S_2O_3^{2-}$, NH_3, NO_2^- or Fe^{2+}) to low redox potential acceptors ($NADP^+$ or NAD^+); the required energy is obtained directly or indirectly from solar radiation or respiration according to species.

Unlike substrate-level phosphorylation, no energy-rich organic intermediates have been detected during either photosynthetic or oxidative phosphorylation, both of which are membrane-bound processes. In each case the membrane establishes a predominantly hydrophobic, rather than an aqueous, environment and imposes a high degree of spatial organization on the constituent redox carriers. Furthermore, its vesicular and largely impermeable nature means that it must contain transport systems which ensure that the supply and removal of substrates, products and cofactors are balanced and also in tune with the cellular demand for ATP. There is, therefore, a basic unity in the nature and organisation of these two types of energy conservation systems which cannot be hidden by their many and obvious differences.

This book will concentrate upon respiration and oxidative phosphorylation; the reader is referred to several excellent, short texts for further discussions of photosynthesis (p. 76).

1.6 Respiration and oxidative phosphorylation

The well-established concept that respiration is catalysed by a highly organized sequence of membrane-bound redox carriers (the *respiratory chain*) arose predominantly from the work of Weiland, Warburg and Keilin in the second and third decades of this century. Weiland, reasoning deductively from examples of organic chemistry, proposed that the oxidation of reduced substrates was achieved by the enzymic removal of hydrogen atoms via the action of *dehydrogenases*, which then spontaneously reduced oxygen to water. On the other hand, Warburg believed that cellular oxidation required the prior activation of oxygen by *atmungsferment* ('respiration enzyme'), later called *cytochrome oxidase* [3]. Keilin's rediscovery of the *cytochrome* system in 1925 largely reconciled these opposing views by providing a link between them (Fig. 1.3). This early view of respiration as a series of linked oxidation–reduction reactions was enhanced by the subsequent discovery of the *nicotinamide nucleotides* (NAD^+ and $NADP^+$) and the *flavin nucleotides* (FMN and FAD) by Warburg, Theorell and others in the early 1930s, and by the demonstration that these redox compounds were associated with dehydrogenase activity. The classical demonstration by Keilin and Hartree in 1939 of the sequential organization of the individual cytochromes, and the much later discoveries of *ubiquinone* and the *iron–sulphur (Fe–S) proteins*, as well as the various *reductases* and other novel redox carriers which characterize the respiratory chains of many anaerobic and chemolithotrophic bacteria, confirmed this view whilst adding greatly to the perceived complexity of the overall process.

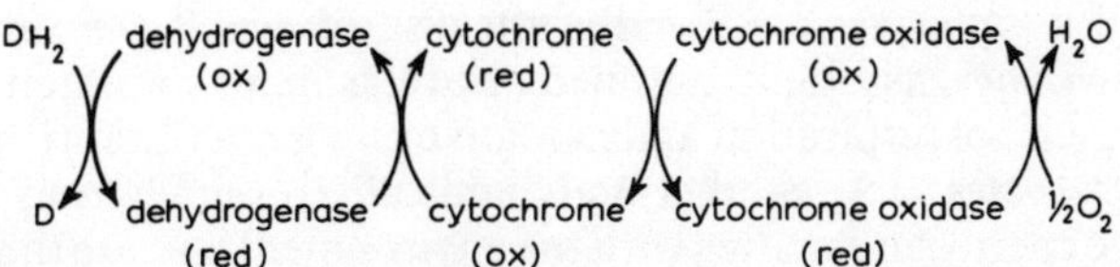

Fig. 1.3 An early view of aerobic respiration.

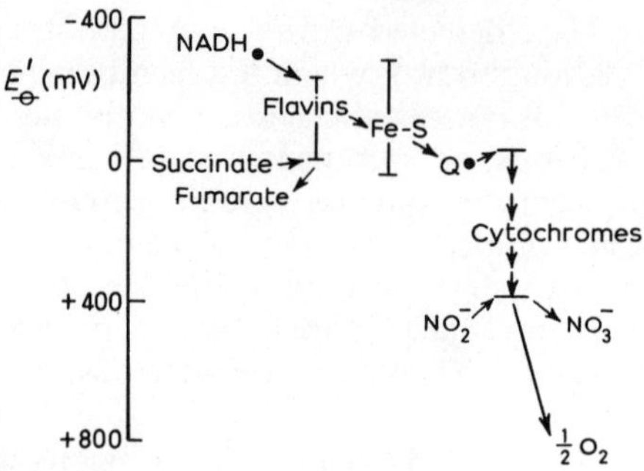

Fig. 1.4 Redox relationships in respiration.

Since these redox components have closely spaced E_m values between approximately -245 mV and $+375$ mV, the transfer of reducing equivalents from the electron donor to the electron acceptor occurs via a series of small redox steps (Fig. 1.4). As a result, the free energy which is available from the overall reaction is released in relatively small packets and hence can be harnessed most efficiently to the endergonic synthesis of ATP from ADP and phosphate. The redox potentials of the donor and acceptor determine both the exact pathway of respiration and also the ATP yield. Thus, the oxidation of NADH ($E'_{\ominus}$ $NAD^+/NADH + H^+ = -320$ mV) occurs via an FMN-linked dehydrogenase, whereas the oxidation of high redox potential substrates such as succinate ($E'_{\ominus}$ fumarate/succinate $= +30$ mV) or nitrite ($E'_{\ominus}$ nitrate/nitrite $= +420$ mV) is independent of NAD^+ and occurs via an FAD-linked dehydrogenase and a specialized cytochrome, respectively. The oxidation of these donors using oxygen as the terminal oxidant ($E'_{\ominus}$ $\frac{1}{2}O_2/H_2O = +820$ mV) is associated with the release of different amounts of free energy ($\Delta G^{\ominus\prime} = -219$, -152 and -77 kJ mol^{-1}, respectively) and hence with different ATP yields. Similarly, the reduction of oxygen is catalysed by cytochrome oxidase, whereas the reduction of, for example, nitrate or fumarate occurs via specialized Mo.Fe–S and FAD-linked reductases, respectively. The reduction of these oxidants by NADH is also associated with the release of different amounts of free energy ($\Delta G^{\ominus\prime} = -219$, -153 and -56 kJ mol^{-1}, respectively) and hence, once again, with different ATP yields.

Two major caveats should be noted at this point. Firstly, $\Delta E'_{\ominus}$ and $\Delta G^{\ominus\prime}$ values refer to standard conditions which clearly do not pertain *in vivo*; under non-standard conditions they are replaced by ΔE_h and ΔG respectively, the values of which can differ quite significantly from their standard counterparts. Secondly, the use of *equilibrium* or *reversible thermodynamics*, as briefly outlined above, is inappropriate to describe the energetics of respiration and oxidative phosphorylation *in vivo* where these processes act as thermodynamically *open systems* (i.e. they exchange energy and matter with the environment and are therefore in a *steady state* rather than at equilibrium). Strictly speaking, *non-*

equilibrium or *irreversible thermodynamics* should be used to describe such processes; unfortunately, however, this approach is too complex to be considered here. The reader is therefore reminded that equilibrium thermodynamics should be restricted to evaluating the individual reactions of these integrated, multi-enzyme processes *in vitro* where they operate as thermodynamically *closed systems*.

The nomenclature of the respiratory chain is based upon the identities of the electron donor and acceptor. Thus the respiratory carriers which catalyse the overall oxidation of NADH, succinate or nitrite by oxygen are known collectively as *NADH oxidase*, *succinate oxidase* and *nitrite oxidase* respectively; when nitrate replaces oxygen, these modified systems are termed *NADH-nitrate reductase* and *succinate-nitrate reductase*. Similarly, those segments of the respiratory chain which catalyse, for example, the reduction of ubiquinone or oxidized cytochrome *c* by NADH are called *NADH-ubiquinone reductase* and *NADH-cytochrome c reductase*, respectively. The traditional terms *NADH dehydrogenase* and *succinate dehydrogenase* are used for the initial oxidation of NADH or succinate by appropriate artificial electron acceptors, and *cytochrome oxidase* is still retained to describe the oxidation of reduced cytochrome *c* by oxygen.

2 The components of the respiratory chain

The respiratory chain of eukaryotic organisms is located on the inner membrane of the mitochondrion (Section 3.1) and principally catalyses the oxidation of NAD(P)H and succinate (together with minor substrates such as glycerol-3-phosphate, fattyacyl-CoA) by molecular oxygen. It is an aggregate of four discrete redox carrier complexes (I, II, III and IV) plus transhydrogenase, ubiquinone and cytochrome *c*. The redox carriers can be monitored by a variety of spectroscopic techniques, and the latter have historically been used to analyse the respiratory membrane *in situ*. These spectroscopic approaches have more recently been supplemented with increasingly sophisticated methods for (i) gently solubilizing the respiratory chain complexes (using either anionic detergents such as cholate or deoxycholate in the presence of KCl, or nonionic detergents such as Triton X-100), (ii) resolving these complexes into their constituent enzymes and redox carriers (using chaotropic agents such as perchlorate), and (iii) investigating the oligomeric nature of many of the apoproteins (using polyacrylamide gel electrophoresis in the presence of dissociating agents such as sodium dodecyl sulphate; SDS-PAGE) [4–9]. It is pertinant at this point, therefore, to examine in some detail the redox and molecular properties of the individual redox carriers and their aggregated complexes, as well as some of the substrates, in order to appreciate fully the complicated nature of the respiratory chain.

2.1 Nicotinamide nucleotides

The nicotinamide nucleotides are NAD^+ (nicotinamide adenine dinucleotide; previously called diphosphopyridine nucleotide or DPN^+) and $NADP^+$ (nicotinamide adenine dinucleotide phosphate; previously called triphosphopyridine nucleotide or TPN^+). $NADP^+$ differs from NAD^+ in that the 2′-hydroxyl group is esterified with phosphoric acid (Fig. 2.1). Both nucleotides act as *coenzymes* for a wide range of soluble dehydrogenases, i.e. they are essential for enzyme activity but are easily dissociated from the apoprotein with the subsequent loss of activity. The redox activities of both coenzymes are attributable to their nicotinamide moieties, which can accept a hydride ion ($H^- \equiv H^+ + 2e^-$). Thus, for example, during the oxidation of malate to oxaloacetate via malate dehydrogenase, NAD^+ accepts H^- and the second proton is lost to the surrounding medium. The reduced forms of the coenzymes are therefore correctly written as NAD(P)H.

$NAD(P)^+$ and NAD(P)H exhibit significantly different absorption spectra, and their oxidation–reduction kinetics can therefore be monitored spectrophotometrically from the change in absorption at 340 nm. The $E'_{\ominus}$ values of the free NAD^+/NADH and $NADP^+$/NADPH couples are −320 and −324 mV, respectively, and are probably not substantially altered by the loose binding to the apoprotein. The

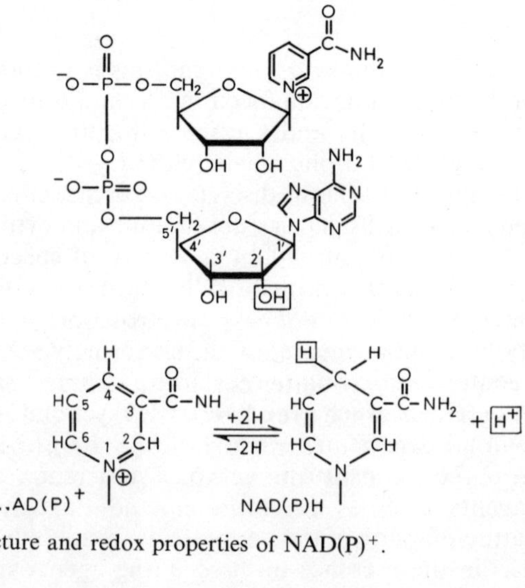

Fig. 2.1 The structure and redox properties of $NAD(P)^+$.

oxidation of many substrates (e.g. glyceraldehyde-3-phosphate, lactate, pyruvate, α-oxoglutarate, malate, β-hydroxyacyl-CoA) by soluble dehydrogenases leads to the formation of NADH; in contrast, relatively few substrates are specific to $NADP^+$ (e.g. glucose-6-phosphate, 6-phosphogluconate) and much of the cellular requirement for NADPH is probably satisfied by the action of the first enzyme of the respiratory chain, viz., nicotinamide nucleotide transhydrogenase.

2.2 Nicotinamide nucleotide transhydrogenase

Nicotinamide nucleotide transhydrogenase [4] consists of two identical peptides (of mol. wt. 120 000) and, unlike the other respiratory chain enzymes or complexes, is devoid of obvious redox centres. It catalyses the reversible transfer of a hydride ion between the 4B-position of NADPH and the 4A-position of NADH:

$$NADPH + H^+ + NAD^+ \rightleftharpoons NADH + H^+ + NADP^+.$$

This reaction, which is specifically inhibited by palmitoyl CoA, is characterized by a considerably higher V_{max} for the oxidation of NADPH than for the reduction of $NADP^+$; the equilibrium constant (K) is very close to unity, since the $E'_{\ominus}$ values of the two couples differ by only 4 mV. However, the work of Ernster and his colleagues has shown that the transhydrogenase reaction is strongly influenced by the energy which is released as a result of either respiration or ATP hydrolysis (see Chapters 4 and 5); both the rate and extent of $NADP^+$ reduction are enhanced (high V_{max}, $K \gg 1$), whereas the oxidation of NADPH is quite strongly inhibited. Energized conditions thus favour the reduction of $NADP^+$ by NADH at the expense of energy, and hence direct reducing equivalents from the predominantly NAD^+-linked dehydrogenases of catabolism towards the predominantly NADPH-oxidizing enzymes of biosynthesis. As a corollory to this, Skulachev has shown that the oxidation of NADPH by NAD^+ can liberate a significant amount of energy *in vitro* under conditions of a high $[NADPH][NAD^+]/[NADP^+][NADH]$ ratio, i.e. where $\Delta E_h \gg 4$ mV. However, since it is extremely doubtful that such a ratio can be maintained *in vivo*, the contribution of the transhydrogenase to respiratory chain phosphorylation is probably negligible.

2.3 Respiratory chain dehydrogenases

The oxidation of NADH, and of primary substrates such as succinate, glycerol-3-phosphate, fatty acyl CoA etc, occurs via specific membrane-bound dehydrogenases. The latter contain a flavin in association with one or more iron–sulphur centres, hence their description originally as *metalloflavoproteins* and more recently as *iron–sulphur flavoproteins*. Although the mechanism of interaction of these two types of redox components *in vivo* is far from clear, a considerable amount is known about their individual properties and functions.

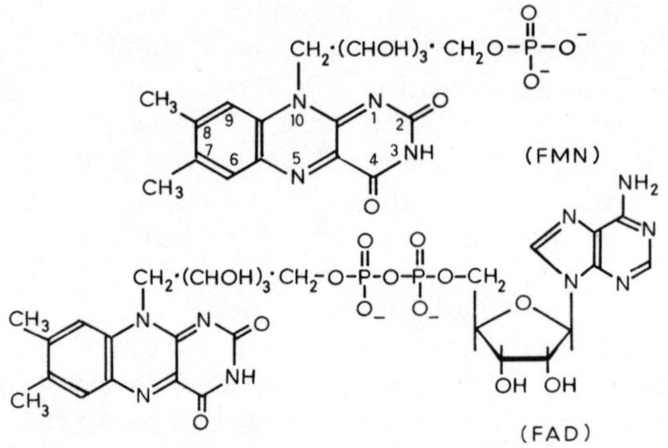

Fig. 2.2 The structures of FMN and FAD.

2.3.1 *Flavoproteins*

Flavoproteins consist of an apoprotein plus either FMN (*flavin mononucleotide*; riboflavin 5′-phosphate) or FAD (*flavin adenine dinucleotide*; Fig. 2.2). Both flavins are tightly bound to the protein and hence act as prosthetic groups rather than coenzymes. The redox properties of the three-ringed isoalloxazine nucleus allow both flavins to carry up to two reducing equivalents ($2H \equiv 2H^+ + 2e^-$), although it is possible that they carry only one equivalent *in vivo*, oscillating between the oxidized and semiquinone forms or the semiquinone and reduced forms (Fig. 2.3). In their oxidized form most flavoproteins exhibit a distinct yellow colour which is due to an absorption band at approximately 450 nm; this band disappears on reduction and they become virtually colourless.

The $E'_{\ominus}$ values of the $FMN/FMNH_2$ and $FAD/FADH_2$ couples are −205 mV and −219 mV, respectively, but these values are often modified when the flavin is bound to the apoprotein. Indeed the wide range of redox potential over which flavoproteins are known to operate *in vivo* enables them to be extremely flexible in their respiratory chain function. Thus lipoyl dehydrogenase reduces NAD^+ at approximately −190 mV, whereas succinate dehydrogenase oxidizes succinate at approximately 0 mV. Although we are concerned here only with the role of flavoproteins as dehydrogenases, it should be noted that some flavoproteins function as oxidases (e.g. in some species of bacteria: $XH_2 + O_2 \longrightarrow X + H_2O_2$) or oxygenases (e.g. various hydroxylases; $RH + NAD(P)H + H^+ + O_2 \rightarrow R.OH + NAD(P)^+ + H_2O$).

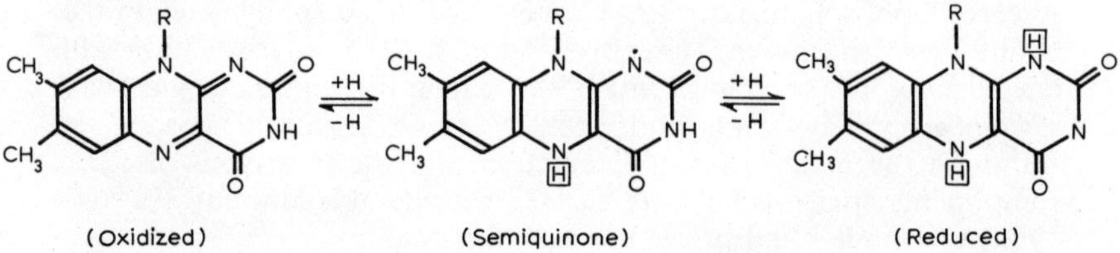

(Oxidized) (Semiquinone) (Reduced)

Fig. 2.3 The redox properties of flavins.

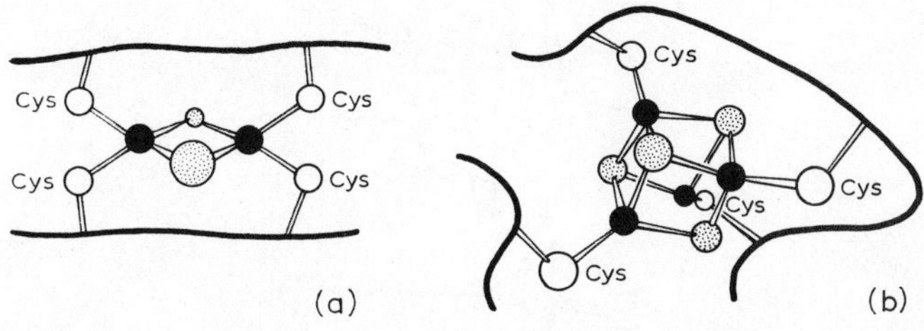

Fig. 2.4 The redox centres of iron – sulphur proteins. (a) [2Fe–2S], and (b) [4Fe–4S]. ●, Fe; ◍, labile-sulphur; ○, cysteine–sulphur.

2.3.2. *Iron–sulphur proteins*

Iron–sulphur proteins (Fe–S proteins; originally called *non-haem iron proteins*) are relatively small (mol. wt. 6–30 000), predominantly hydrophilic redox carriers which contain either 2, 4 or 8 atoms each of iron and 'labile-sulphur' [10]. They are frequently membrane-bound but are fairly easily extracted, and a large number have been purified since the original isolation by Mortenson in 1962 of ferredoxin from the obligately anaerobic bacterium *Clostridium pasteurianum*. [2Fe–2S] proteins are characterized by a redox centre which contains two iron atoms that are held in a lattice composed of four atoms of cysteine-sulphur and two atoms of 'labile-sulphur' (Fig. 2.4a); the latter are so named since, unlike the cysteine-sulphurs, they are readily released as H_2S under acid conditions, with a resultant loss of redox function. [4Fe–4S] proteins differ from their [2Fe–2S] counterparts by having a redox centre with cubane-type geometry in which four iron atoms form a cube with four atoms of labile-sulphur, the cube being held in place by four cysteine-sulphurs (Fig. 2.4b). [8Fe–8S] proteins, more correctly described as 2[4Fe–4S] proteins, contain two separate [4Fe–4S] centres. [2Fe–2S] and [4Fe–4S] proteins function in respiration and green plant photosynthesis, whereas 2[4Fe–4S] proteins are predominantly associated with fermentative metabolism; all three types are involved in nitrogen fixation and bacterial photosynthesis.

All of the iron–sulphur proteins absorb in the 450–500 nm region of the spectrum, albeit rather diffusely, and like the nicotinamide nucleotides and flavins show diminished absorption when reduced. Reductive titration indicates that the [2Fe–2S] and [4Fe–4S] proteins carry only one electron, whereas 2[4Fe–4S] proteins carry two (one at each redox centre). The mechanism of electron carriage is complicated and probably involves extensive electron delocalization between the iron atoms which constitute the centre; the majority of iron–sulphur proteins are unable to carry protons. Reduction of most iron–sulphur proteins causes the charge at the redox centre to decrease from (2 +) to (1 +), although the reduction of some types of [4Fe–4S] proteins (originally called *high potential iron proteins* or *HIPIP*) is accompanied by a decrease in charge from (3 +) to (2 +). Since the (3 +) and (1 +) oxidation states contain an unpaired electron, whereas the

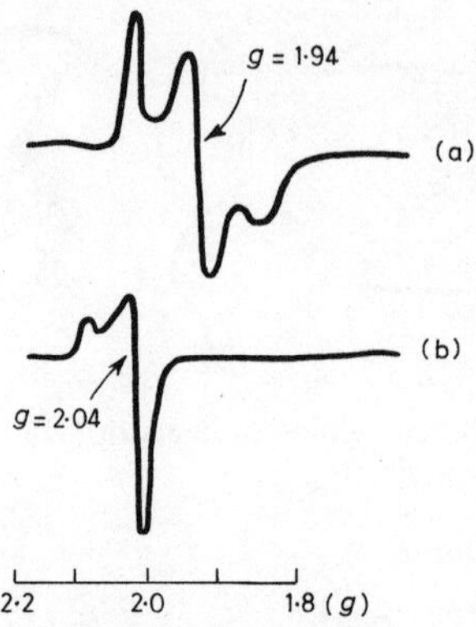

Fig. 2.5 First derivative EPR spectra of iron–sulphur proteins. (a) oxidation state (1 +), and (b) oxidation state (3 +) (after Hall *et al.*, 1975).

(2 +) oxidation state does not (*paramagnetic* and *diamagnetic* states respectively), the nature and redox state of an unknown iron–sulphur protein is easily determined using *electron paramagnetic resonance* (EPR) *spectroscopy* to monitor the presence of the paramagnetic species. In this technique the sample is placed between the poles of a magnet at ≤ 77 K, and the absorption of a constant microwave frequency is measured as a function of the magnetic field strength. The resultant EPR spectrum is characterized by the value of g (the *spectroscopic splitting factor*), which is proportional to the amount of energy required to reverse the spin of the unpaired electron, and is thus a function of the microwave frequency and the magnetic field strength; the (3 +) and (1 +) oxidation states exhibit different g values (Fig. 2.5). The E_m values of the iron–sulphur proteins range from -600 to $+350$ mV, but the precise factors which determine these values have yet to be resolved.

2.3.3 *NADH dehydrogenase and complex I*

NADH dehydrogenase has proved one of the most difficult of the respiratory chain components to purify. However, a soluble, low molecular weight form of the enzyme (mol. wt. 70 000) that catalyses the oxidation of NADH by exogenous ubiquinone has recently been described by Hatefi. It is an iron–sulphur flavoprotein which contains one molecule each of FMN, [2Fe–2S] and [4Fe–4s] distributed on three peptide subunits. Similarly, Ragan has isolated a separate iron–sulphur protein which also contains three major peptides. It is clear, however, that these preparations are only fragments of a larger complex (*NADH-Q reductase* or *complex I*; mol. wt. $\geq 600\,000$) which is composed of at least 17 peptides and contains not less than 16 irons and labile-sulphurs, plus FMN, ubiquinone and phospholipid [5,6]. The activities of NADH dehydrogenase and complex I are both inhibited by rhein, rotenone and piericidin A (Fig. 2.6).

EPR spectroscopy of mammalian and yeast respiratory membranes

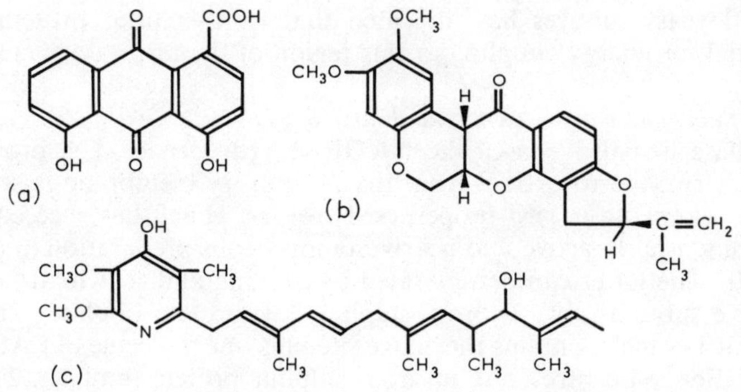

Fig. 2.6 Inhibitors of complex I. (a) Rhein, (b) rotenone, and (c) piericidin A.

has indicated the presence of five different iron–sulphur centres (of both the [2Fe–2S] and [4Fe–4S] types) which are attributable to complex I. The separate centres are detected by a now classical procedure which entails poising the membranes at a series of different E_h values at room temperature, then freezing them rapidly and measuring the EPR spectrum; the E_h at which the characteristic signal for each iron–sulphur centre attains half its maximum height is equal to the E_m of that particular centre (Fig. 2.7). The results clearly indicate large differences between centre *N*-1a (E_m − 380 mV), centres *N*-1b, *N*-3, *N*-4 ($E_m \cong$ − 245 mV) and centre *N*-2 (E_m − 20 mV). Since spectrophotometric studies indicate that FMN probably acts close to NADH and the group of medium E_m centres, and that ATP causes the reduction of FMN concomitant with the oxidation of N-2, it appears fairly certain that electron transfer over the span (FMN, *N*-1b, *N*-3, *N*-4) → *N*-2 leads to the release of sufficient energy to drive the synthesis of ATP. Centre *N*-1a is probably not in equilibrium with the rest of the respiratory chain, and its function is uncertain. Rather unusually, centres *N*-1a and *N*-2 appear each to carry a proton. The sites of inhibition by rotenone and piericidin A are probably close to the junction of *N*-2 and ubiquinone, whereas rhein binds to the active site of the enzyme. Multiple iron–sulphur proteins have also been detected in membrane-bound NADH dehydrogenases from various species of plant mitochondria and bacteria. The elegant work of Garland and his colleagues using iron- or sulphate-

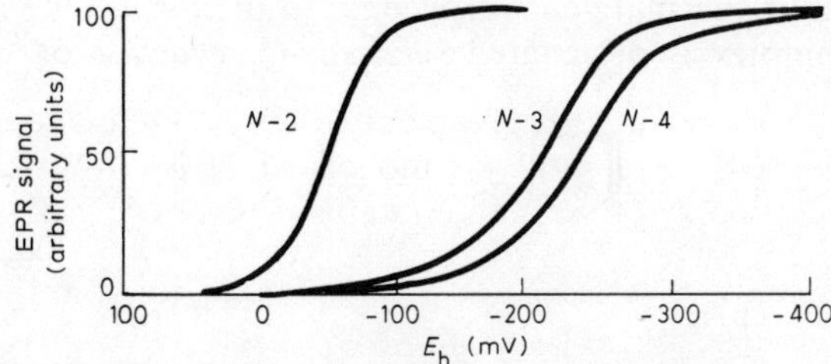

Fig. 2.7 Potentiometric titrations of iron–sulphur centres in complex I.

limited yeast cultures has indicated that iron–sulphur proteins are essential for energy coupling in this region of the respiratory chain.

2.3.4 *Succinate dehydrogenase and complex II*

Succinate dehydrogenase, like NADH dehydrogenase, has proved a difficult enzyme to extract from the respiratory membrane in a form which retains its *in vivo* properties. However, Hatefi has succeeded in purifying a fairly active and nearly homogeneous preparation (mol. wt. 97 000). The latter can be separated by freezing and thawing into two inactive subunits, viz. an iron–sulphur flavoprotein (mol. wt. 70 000; subunit 1) which contains the active site plus one molecule of FAD and two [2Fe–2S] centres, and an iron–sulphur protein (mol. wt. 27 000; subunit 2) which contains a [4Fe–4S] centre but no flavin. Amino acid sequencing indicates that the flavin is covalently bound to the apoprotein via a histidine residue (8-N3 histidyl-FAD), whereas in many flavoproteins the flavin is bound ionically via its negatively charged phosphate groups. The reason for covalent bonding is probably that it raises the standard redox potential of the FAD/$FADH_2$ couple from that of the free form (-219 mV) to about that of the fumarate/succinate couple ($+30$ mV), thus facilitating the action of succinate dehydrogenase. Interestingly, covalent bonding of FAD to a histidyl residue also occurs in fumarate reductase, the enzyme which reduces fumarate to succinate and hence enables some species of bacteria to grow anaerobically using fumarate as a terminal electron acceptor for respiration in place of molecular oxygen.

EPR spectroscopy of membrane-bound succinate dehydrogenase has confirmed the presence of three iron–sulphur centres, viz. S-1 and S-2 (E_m $+15$ mV and -260 mV respectively) which are associated with subunit 1, and S-3 (E_m $+60$ mV) on subunit 2. Electron transfer through succinate dehydrogenase therefore probably occurs in the sequence (FAD, S-1)$\rightarrow$S-3; the measured E_m value of S-2, like that of N-1a, is presumably too low to allow this centre to be catalytically active, and its function is currently unclear.

It should be noted that purified succinate dehydrogenase is able to catalyse the reduction of a variety of artificial electron acceptors, but not ubiquinone. Reduction of the latter requires the additional presence of cytochrome b_{558} and a smaller peptide (subunits 3 and 4), which also serve to anchor succinate dehydrogenase to the membrane *in vivo*; the resultant complex is designated *succinate-Q reductase* or *complex II*.

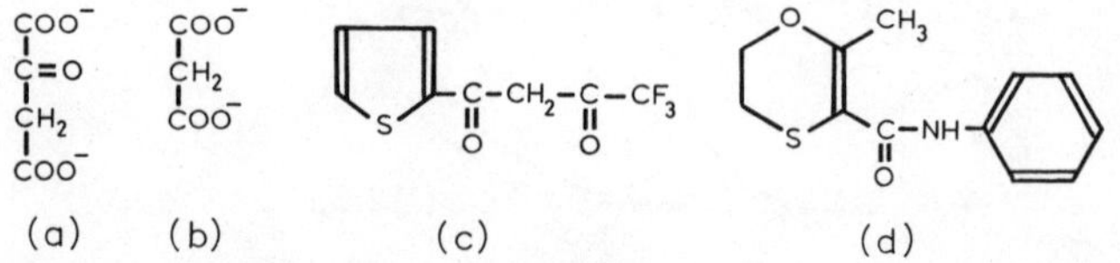

Fig. 2.8 Inhibitors of complex II. (a) oxaloacetate, (b) malonate, (c) thenoyltrifluoroacetone (TTFA), and (d) carboxin.

The activity of the latter is inhibited by oxaloacetate, malonate, thenoyltrifluoroacetone and carboxin (Fig. 2.8); oxaloacetate and malonate bind competitively with succinate at the active site of the enzyme, whereas the other two inhibitors prevent electron transfer from S-3 to ubisemiquinone and are therefore ineffective against purified succinate dehydrogenase [6.7].

2.4 Ubiquinone

Ubiquinone (or coenzyme Q) was discovered independently in 1957 by Morton and Crane. It consists of a substituted 1,4-benzoquinone nucleus which contains a long polyisoprenoid side-chain at C-6 (Fig. 2.9); the latter consists of 6-12 isoprene units according to source, 10 units being present in ubiquinone from mammalian sources (Q-10). The redox properties of ubiquinone lie in the ability of its nucleus to accept 2H and form ubiquinol, probably via a semiquinone ($Q \rightarrow QH\cdot \rightarrow QH_2$). The original observations that ubiquinone could be readily extracted from respiratory membranes using organic solvents, and that it could be purified by adsorption or thin-layer chromatography under non-aqueous conditions, suggested that it was entirely lipid in nature. However, evidence has recently been presented which indicates that it is bound to protein *in vivo*, possibly as a series of quinone pairs each of which is associated with a hydrophobic subunit in complex I, II and/or III [8].

Unlike the other components of the respiratory chain, ubiquinone absorbs principally in the near ultraviolet region of the spectrum. On reduction to quinol, the major absorption band at 272 nm decreases in intensity and shifts to approximately 290 nm, thus allowing the oxidation–reduction kinetics of the carrier *in situ* to be monitored spectrophotometrically. This technically difficult operation was first achieved in 1961 by Chance and Redfearn who observed reduction of ubiquinone by NADH or succinate, and reoxidation of ubiquinol by molecular oxygen. This redox role for ubiquinone was strongly supported by the later extraction–reactivation studies of Sarcowska, Ernster and others; in these experiments the quinone was extracted gently from lyophilized respiratory membranes using non-polar organic solvents such as *n*-pentane (with the parallel loss of both NADH and succinate oxidase activities), and then added back in the correct concentrations to the depleted membranes (with the resultant reappearance of these activities). Subsequent controversy over whether the

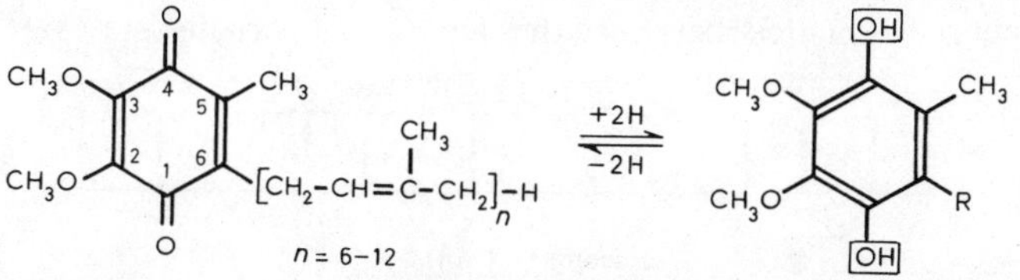

Fig. 2.9 The structure and redox properties of ubiquinone.

oxidation–reduction kinetics of ubiquinone were sufficiently fast to allow it to act as an obligatory, main-chain carrier was later settled by Klingenberg who showed unambiguously that it collects reducing equivalents from the various dehydrogenases and passes them on to the terminal cytochrome system. This function is perfectly compatible with its very high molar concentration relative to the other respiratory chain components and with its E_m values (E_mQ/QH· $\simeq -150$ mV; E_mQH·/QH$_2$ $\simeq +150$ mV).

2.5 Cytochromes

The cytochromes were discovered by MacMunn in 1884 during spectroscopic studies of thin tissue slices. However, the four-banded spectrum was confused with that of myoglobin and, after some acrimonious discussion with Hoppe-Seyler, the discovery was forgotten. They were rediscovered in 1925 by Keilin [11] who reported that the flight muscles of certain insects exhibited the characteristic four-banded spectrum which could be differentially enhanced or diminished by exposure to reducing or oxidizing agents. Further studies using a primitive microspectroscope indicated that three of the bands (a, b and c) could be attributed to the α-bands of separate *a*-, *b*- and *c*-type cytochromes, whereas the fourth band (d) was composed of the fused β-bands of these cytochromes. The dense absorption at the blue end of the spectrum was attributed to the overlapping γ- or Soret-bands (Fig. 2.10). Later, Warburg showed that the *a*-type cytochrome was a composite of cytochromes a and a_3; since cytochrome a_3 reacts with molecular oxygen and is structurally and physically closely related to cytochrome *a*, the two cytochromes are together called *cytochrome oxidase*. The *c*-type cytochrome was subsequently shown to be comprised of physically separate cytochromes c and c_1, and in the last few years sophisticated spectrophotometric and potentiometric analyses of the *b*-type cytochrome have indicated the presence of two components, viz. cytochrome b_{562} (also called b_K, after Keilin) and cytochrome b_{566} (also called b_T, since it was once regarded as being directly involved in energy transduction; the absorption spectrum of this cytochrome has a strong shoulder at 558 nm).

The cytochromes each consist of a *haem* prosthetic group bound to a protein, the individual cytochromes differing principally in the nature of their substituent groups at C-2, C-4, C-5 and C-8 of the haem (Fig. 2.11). The latter is composed of *porphyrin* (four pyrrole rings joined by methenyl bridges) plus a central iron atom which carries a single electron and hence oscillates between the ferric and ferrous states (Fe^{3+} +

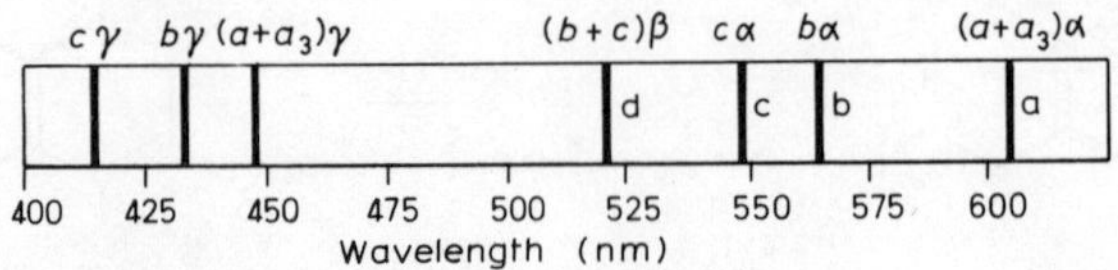

Fig. 2.10 Cytochrome spectral bands.

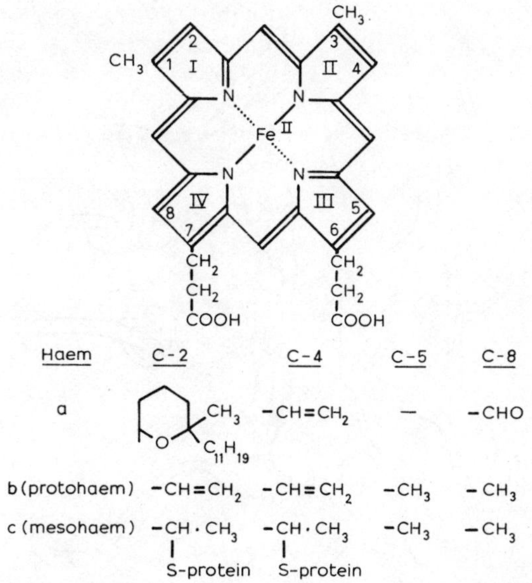

Haem	C-2	C-4	C-5	C-8
a	(ring) CH_3, $C_{11}H_{19}$	$-CH{=}CH_2$	—	$-CHO$
b (protohaem)	$-CH{=}CH_2$	$-CH{=}CH_2$	$-CH_3$	$-CH_3$
c (mesohaem)	$-CH\cdot CH_3$ (S-protein)	$-CH\cdot CH_3$ (S-protein)	$-CH_3$	$-CH_3$

Fig. 2.11 Haem structures.

$e^- \rightleftharpoons Fe^{2+}$). Iron is a transition element of outer electronic structure $3d^6 4s^2$; ferrous iron ($3d^6$) and ferric iron ($3d^5$) may therefore exist in high-spin or low-spin states (Fig. 2.12). In most cytochromes, unlike haemoglobin, the iron is forced into the low-spin state; six orbitals therefore remain unfilled (two in 3d, one in 4s and three in 4p) and the iron can thus bind six ligands in an octohedral co-ordination complex. The lone pair electrons of the four pyrrole-N are eminently suited to this role and serve to hold the iron roughly within the plane of the porphyrin ring; the axial co-ordination positions 5 and 6 are available for bonding to suitable ligands in the peptide (e.g. His-N, Met-S). Interestingly, cytochromes *a* and a_3 can exist in both the high-spin and low-spin states; in cytochrome a_3, an axial co-ordination position is free and can be occupied by a variety of weak ligands such as water, oxygen or carbon monoxide. The E_m values of the individual cytochromes are dictated by structural considerations; thus, E_m varies inversely with the electrostatic charge on the axial ligands (His-N > Met-S > water) and, to a lesser extent, with the degree of unsaturation of the ring substituents (vinyl > thioether) such that E_m *b*-type < *c*-type < *a*-type.

Cytochromes b_{562} (E_m + 40 mV and + 120 mV) and b_{566} (E_m − 34 mV) are extremely hydrophobic and are firmly embedded in the

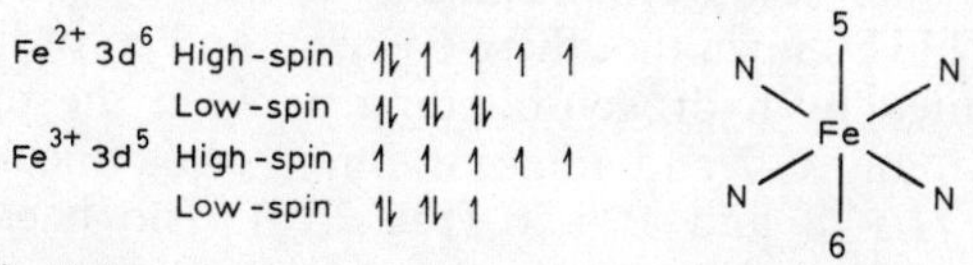

Fe^{2+} $3d^6$	High-spin	↑↓ ↑ ↑ ↑ ↑
	Low-spin	↑↓ ↑↓ ↑↓
Fe^{3+} $3d^5$	High-spin	↑ ↑ ↑ ↑ ↑
	Low-spin	↑↓ ↑↓ ↑

Fig. 2.12 Iron spin states.

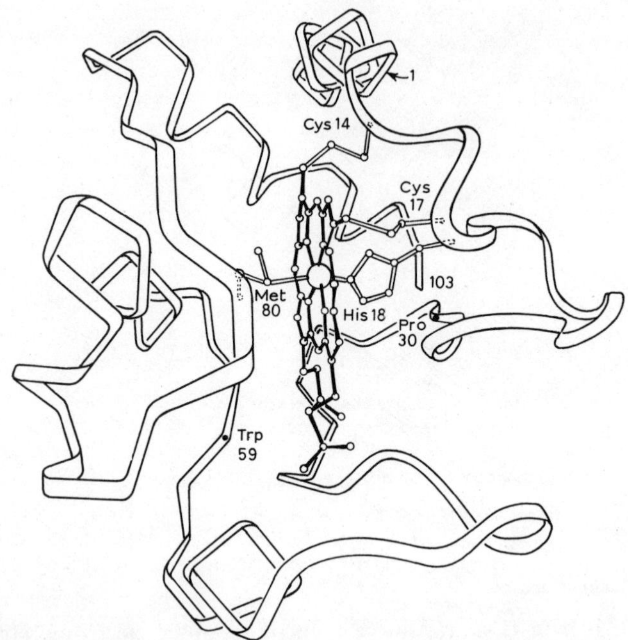

Fig. 2.13 The structure of cytochrome *c* (the ball in the centre of the molecule represents the iron atom) (after Salemme, 1977).

membrane. Substantial progress has recently been made towards the extraction and purification of the *b*-type cytochromes. There is some evidence that cytochromes b_{562} and b_{566} exist as a dimer of two peptides (of mol. wt. 30 000), each of which binds a single protohaem; the different absorption maxima and E_m values of the haems probably reflect their respective environments. Interestingly, each monomer is probably capable of carrying a proton as well as an electron. The E_m value of cytochrome b_{566}, but not of the other *b*-type cytochrome, is substantially increased following energization of the membrane by ATP (E_m − 34 mV → + 240 mV).

In contrast, cytochrome *c* (mol. wt. 12 600; E_m + 260 mV) is very easy to purify since it is extremely hydrophilic and is only loosely bound to the membrane [12]. Haem *c* is attached to the protein both covalently (via thioether cysteine bridges from the C-2 and C-4 residues of the haem to Cys-14 and Cys-17, respectively) and co-ordinately (via the imidazole-N of His-18 and the sulphur of Met-80). The elegant 2.8 Å X-ray diffraction analyses of cytochrome *c* carried out by Dickerson and his colleagues have shown that these covalent and co-ordinate linkages are supplemented by hydrogen-bonding between the propionic acid moieties at C-6 and C-7 and adjacent amino acids (including Trp-59), and between His-18 and Pro-30 (Fig. 2.13). The haem is inserted sideways into a hydrophobic crevice within the peptide such that only the outer edges of pyrrole rings II, and to a lesser extent III, are exposed. The surface of the molecule is highly charged and exhibits distinct areas which are cationic or anionic. Cationic residues, mostly lysines, surround the haem edge at the 'top' and 'front' of the molecule and are responsible for binding cytochrome *c* in an ordered manner to its neighbours, cytochromes c_1 and aa_3. The overlapping nature of the two binding sites suggests that in order to effect electron transfer, cytochrome *c* must be capable of some mobility within the membrane; electron transfer into and out of the central iron atom of cytochrome *c* probably occurs via pyrrole ring II. Cytochrome c_1 is rather more firmly bound to the respiratory membrane, but it has recently been solubilized and purified by King. It is a relatively large cytochrome (mol. wt. 45 000; E_m + 225 mV) and is comprised of two subunits, the larger of which binds a single haem *c*.

Cytochromes b_{562}, b_{566} and c_1, together with a [2Fe–2S] protein (mol. wt. 26 000; E_m + 260 mV) which was discovered by Rieske in 1964, constitute *ubiquinol-cytochrome c reductase* or *complex III* (mol. wt. 250 000). The latter contains seven different subunits, amongst which are two 'core' peptides (subunits 1 and 2) that are not associated with any redox centres. Electron transfer through complex III appears to be extremely complicated, and probably entails some form of cyclic flow. It is inhibited by the antibiotics antimycin A and 2-heptyl-4-hydroxyquinoline-N-oxide (HQNO), but the exact sites of action of these inhibitors have yet to be determined.

Cytochrome oxidase (cytochrome aa_3 or *complex IV*) is the terminal enzyme of the respiratory chain. In its purified state (mol. wt. 140 000) it contains 2 molecules each of haem *a* and copper, and is composed of seven subunits plus phospholipid [9, 13]. The two haems function as spectrally distinct entities, viz. *a* and a_3, which differ in their redox properties (E_m + 230 mV and + 375 mV, respectively) and in the nature of their axial ligands. The two copper atoms, Cu_A and Cu_B (E_m + 245 mV and + 340 mV), act like the cytochromes as one-electron carriers ($Cu^{2+} + e^- \rightleftharpoons Cu^+$). All four redox centres are associated with subunits 1 and 2. Ferricytochrome *a* and cupric Cu_A are paramagnetic and hence are detectable by EPR spectroscopy; in contrast, Cu_B is antiferromagnetically coupled to cytochrome a_3 at the active site of the enzyme and is therefore 'invisible'. Cytochrome oxidase activity is readily inhibited by carbon monoxide, cyanide (CN^-) and azide (N_3^-).

In 1926 Warburg first showed that the ability of carbon monoxide to inhibit respiration could be reversed by light, which dissociates the oxidase Fe^{2+}·CO complex and allows the free enzyme to reduce molecular oxygen [3]. When this photoalleviation of inhibition (measured as increased respiratory activity) is plotted as a function of the wavelength of the relieving light, the resultant *photochemical action spectrum* closely resembles the absorption spectrum of the a_3^{2+}·CO complex and thus indicates that cytochrome a_3 is the terminal redox component of the respiratory chain. This method, and the measurement

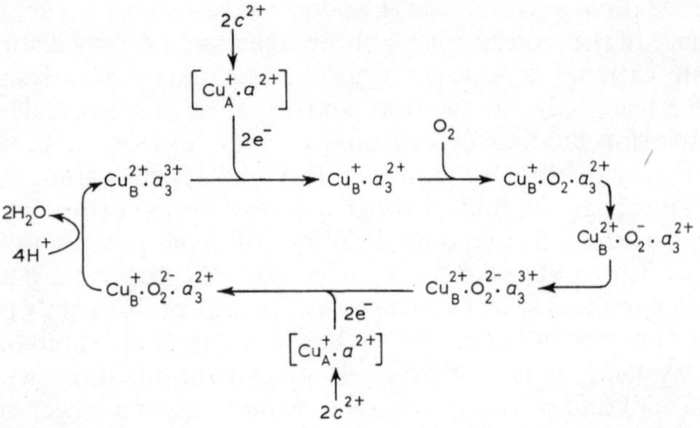

Fig. 2.14 The reaction cycle of cytochrome oxidase (after Clore *et al.*, 1980).

of redox kinetics by flash photolysis and rapid-flow spectrophotometry, are now the classical procedures for determining whether a redox carrier can act as a competent terminal oxidase. In contrast to carbon monoxide, both cyanide and azide inhibit respiration by combining optimally with the oxidized form of cytochrome a_3; neither oxygen or any of the above inhibitors react significantly with cytochrome *a*.

The terminal stage of respiration can be represented by the equation:

$$4H^+ + 4e^- + O_2 \longrightarrow 2H_2O.$$

The electrons are provided via the sequential oxidation of four molecules of ferrocytochrome *c*, whereas the protons are drawn from the aqueous environment. Low-temperature kinetic studies, carried out mainly in the laboratories of Chance and Malmström using highly sophisticated optical and EPR spectroscopy, have recently indicated that cytochrome oxidase participates in a complex reaction cycle which involves a series of well-defined redox intermediates (Fig. 2.14). Starting with the oxidase in its fully oxidized state ($Cu_A^{2+} \cdot a^{3+} \cdot Cu_B^{2+} \cdot a_3^{3+}$), the first part of the cycle involves the formation of the reduced species $Cu_A^+ \cdot a^{2+}$ at the expense of two molecules of ferrocytochrome *c*, followed by the further transfer of these two electrons to the active site of the oxidase, i.e. to form $Cu_B^+ \cdot a_3^{2+}$. The latter then binds a molecule of oxygen to produce an oxygenated bridge complex which undergoes successive internal electron transfers to form a bound peroxide of very high standard redox potential ($Cu_B^{2+} \cdot O_2^{2-} \cdot a_3^{3+}$; $E_m \geq +700$ mV). This complex subsequently receives two more electrons from ferrocytochrome *c*, via $Cu_A^+ \cdot a^{2+}$, and finally reacts with $4H^+$ to yield two molecules of water and to regenerate the oxidase in its fully oxidized state. It should be noted that at no time during this reaction cycle does the oxidase become fully reduced ($Cu_A^+ \cdot a^{2+} \cdot Cu_B^+ \cdot a_3^{2+}$); instead, it passes to and from the fully oxidized state via a family of oxygenated and non-oxygenated, mixed-valence-state intermediates.

An entirely different cytochrome oxidase terminates respiration in

Table 2.1 The composition of the respiratory chain

Component	*Mol. wt.*	*Molar ratio*	*Redox centres*	*Peptides*
Transhydrogenase	240 000	1		1
Complex I	600 000	1	FMN, 5Fe-S,Q	17
Complex II	117 000	1	FAD, 3Fe-S, $b_{558(566)}$	4
Ubiquinone	860	16	Q	2
Complex III	250 000	1	b_{562}, b_{566}, c_1, Fe-S	7
Cytochrome *c*	12 600	2	*c*	1
Complex IV	140 000	2	*a*, Cu_A, Cu_B, a_3	7

some protozoa, viz. cytochrome *d*. The latter is a fairly common oxidase in bacteria, but is encountered only rarely in eukaryotes. Haem *d* (dihydroporphyrin or chlorin) differs from protohaem in that the C-2 vinyl residue is replaced by -CHOH·R, and pyrrole ring IV is more reduced. Cytochrome *d* contains two haem *d* (E_m + 245 and + 345 mV), plus two coppers (in protozoa) or plus two haem *b* (in bacteria).

2.6 The composition and reconstitution of the respiratory chain

The immense complexity of the respiratory chain becomes apparent when it is realized that the oxidation of NADPH and succinate by molecular oxygen requires the presence of 21 different redox centres and up to 39 different peptides (Table 2.1). When the known multiplicity of certain components is taken into account, it is possible that a single respiratory chain unit (mol. wt. approx. 1.52×10^6) contains as many as 41 redox centres and 47 peptides, together with significant amounts of phospholipid which assist with the maintenance of membrane integrity and organization.

One of the classical methods of investigating a multicomponent reaction, of which respiration is a prime example, is to separate the individual components and then attempt to reconstitute the original system in an active from by mixing the components together in the correct proportions. This approach was successfully applied to the respiratory chain in 1961 by Hatefi, who reconstituted firstly NADH oxidase from complexes I, III, IV and cytochrome *c*, and then succinate oxidase from complexes II, III, IV, ubiquinone and cytochrome *c*; the reconstituted systems exhibited high activities which were fully sensitive to appropriate inhibitors. Reconstitution of respiratory chain complexes from their constituent redox carriers has been less successful, although an active complex II has recently been reconstituted from succinate dehydrogenase and cytochrome b_{558} in the presence of the anti-chaotropic ions, sulphate or phosphate, and D_2O; reconstitution of complexes I, III and IV has not yet been achieved.

2.7 Spectrophotometric analyses

Since most of the respiratory chain components exhibit slightly different absorption characteristics in their oxidized and reduced forms, their

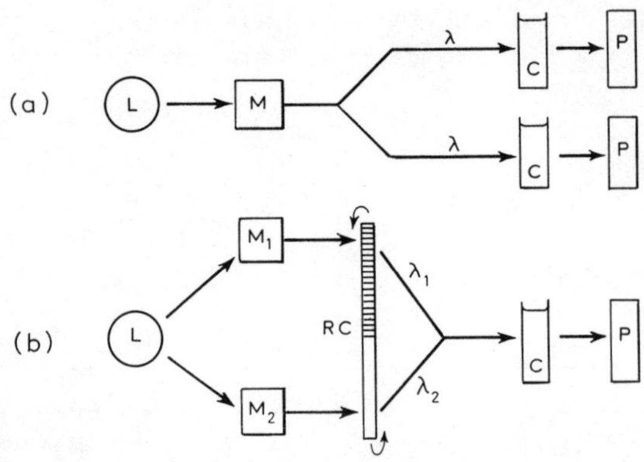

Fig. 2.15 The principles of (a) split-beam, and (b) dual-wavelength spectrophotometry. Abbreviations: L, light source; M, monochromator; RC, rotating chopper; C, cuvette; P, photomultiplier.

redox states can readily be determined by spectrophotometric procedures based on either a *split-beam* or a *dual-wavelength spectrophotometer* (Fig. 2.15). The former utilizes a monochromatic light beam of variable wavelength which is subsequently split and passed through two cuvettes, one containing the solution and the other the solvent; the result is the *absolute absorption spectrum* of the solute. When the absolute spectra of, for example, reduced and oxidized cytochrome *c* are compared, their slight differences in absorption are easily seen (Fig. 2.16a). These differences can be made even more obvious by placing ferrocytochrome *c* in one cuvette and ferricytochrome *c* in the other, and recording the resultant *reduced minus oxidized difference spectrum* (Fig. 2.16b). This technique is particularly useful for detecting and quantifying low concentrations of redox carriers under conditions where it is virtually impossible to measure absolute spectra, e.g. when turbid suspensions of mitochondria or bacteria are employed.

In the visible region, the succinate *reduced minus oxidized* difference spectrum of respiratory membranes contains contributions from most of the redox carriers (Fig. 2.17). Thus the individual cytochromes are seen as positive inflections (since reduced cytochrome absorbs more strongly than oxidized cytochrome), whereas the flavoproteins and iron–sulphur proteins are seen as a combined negative inflection (since both of these carriers absorb more strongly in their oxidized forms). Note that in this particular preparation the *b*-type cytochrome is largely hidden by the strong absorption of the *c*- and *a*-type cytochromes; however, following the addition of antimycin A the absorption of the *b*-type cytochrome becomes immediately apparent whereas that of the other cytochromes essentially disappears. This effect is caused by antimycin A effectively inhibiting respiration between the *b*-type cytochromes and cytochrome c_1 (the effect of antimycin A on the reduction levels of the individual *b*-type cytochromes is extremely complicated and need not be considered

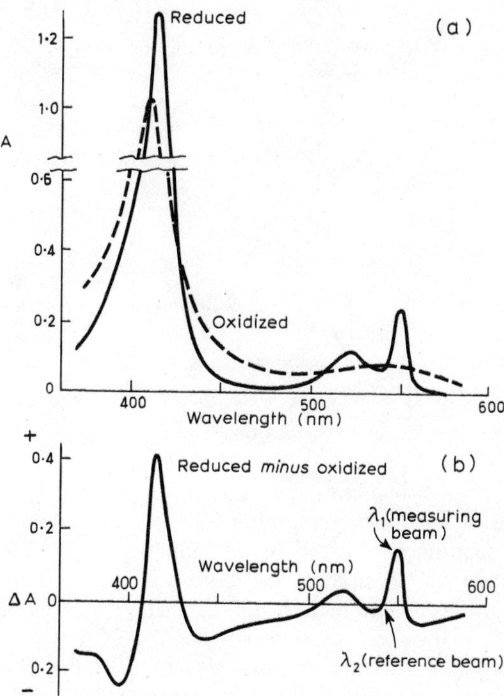

Fig. 2.16 Absorption spectra of cytochrome *c*. (a) Absolute spectra, and (b) reduced minus oxidized difference spectrum.

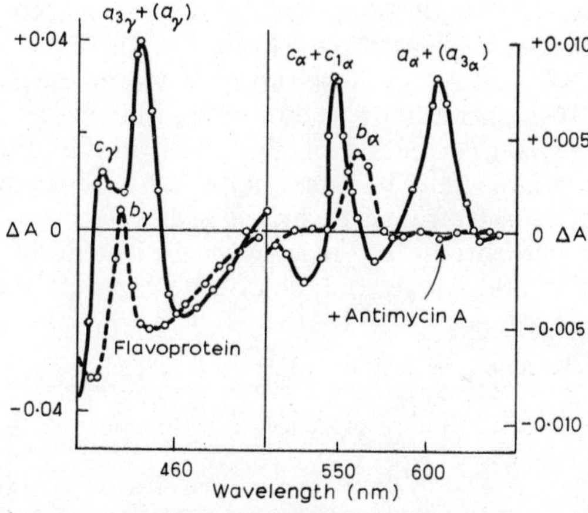

Fig. 2.17 Reduced *minus* oxidized difference spectrum of the mammalian respiratory chain (after Chance, 1956).

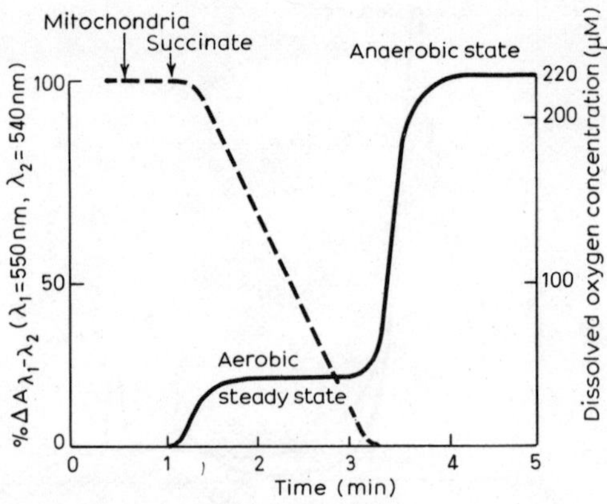

Fig. 2.18 The reduction kinetics of cytochrome *c in situ.*

here). Such a *crossover point* is caused by the redox components on the substrate side of the block remaining fully reduced, whilst those on the oxygen side become reoxidized (since reducing equivalents flow out to oxygen without being replenished from succinate). This technique is used to determine the site of action of inhibitors and/or the sequence of redox carriers within the respiratory chain.

Since many experiments require the measurement of oxidation–reduction changes in individual redox carriers using very small samples of membrane, the absorption changes are correspondingly slight and can only be monitored accurately using a dual wavelength spectrophotometer. The latter contains a single cuvette through which alternatively pass two monochromatic light beams of slightly different wavelength (λ_1 and λ_2 of Fig. 2.16b); since these wavelengths are close together and only one sample is used, errors resulting from artefactual turbidity changes are minimized. Using this approach it is possible to measure the oxidation–reduction kinetics of cytochrome *c in situ* (Fig. 2.18). Following the addition of succinate to respiratory membranes, oxygen uptake rapidly attains a maximum rate but cytochrome *c* is only partially reduced (i.e. a small percentage of the total is in the ferrous state, the remainder stays as ferric). The extent of its reduction is governed by the rate of electron transfer from cytochrome c_1 and the rate constant for its oxidation by cytochrome *a*; since both the extent of reduction of cytochrome *c* and the oxygen uptake rate are constant, the cytochrome

Table 2.2 Aerobic steady state reduction levels

Substrate	*% reduction*			
	Fp	*b* (total)	$c_1 + c$	aa_3
Succinate	40	25	19	4

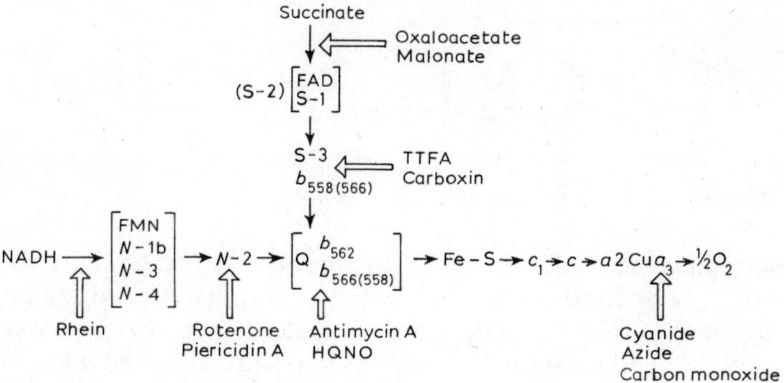

Fig. 2.19 The mitochondrial respiratory chain.

is said to be in the *aerobic steady state.* Only when the concentration of dissolved oxygen becomes so low that it limits the rate of respiration does cytochrome *c* become fully reduced and enter the *anaerobic state.* The percentage reduction of redox carriers in the aerobic steady state decreases as the oxygen end of the respiratory chain is approached (Table 2.2), and hence this value can be used to determine the approximate position of individual carriers in the chain. The latter can also be achieved by comparing the reoxidation kinetics of individual carriers, on a millisecond time-scale, following the addition of oxygen to anaerobic membranes; those carriers nearest the end of the chain become reoxidized first (e.g. cytochrome aa_3 is oxidized before cytochrome *c*).

From a consideration of redox potential measurements, oxidation–reduction kinetics, inhibitor studies and extraction–reactivation experiments described above, the respiratory chain carriers are currently thought to operate in the sequence shown in Fig. 2.19.

Interestingly, the mitochondrial respiratory chains of higher plants and some yeasts are branched at the level of ubiquinone. The alternative pathway to oxygen is resistant to inhibition by cyanide, but is readily inhibited by metal-chelating agents, particularly salicylhydroxamic acid (SHAM). The redox carriers involved in this pathway have not been unambiguously identified, but autoxidizable forms of ubiquinone and/or an Fe–S protein are the prime candidates.

2.8 Bacterial respiratory chains

Bacteria do not contain mitochondria. Instead, their respiratory chains are located on the *cytoplasmic* (*plasma*) *membrane* which comprises part of the cell envelope.

The aerobic respiratory chains of chemoheterotrophic bacteria contain the same basic types of redox carriers as are present in mitochondria, i.e. Fe–S flavoproteins, quinones, cytochromes and cytochrome oxidases. However, on closer examination a number of important differences can be observed; these are usually typified either

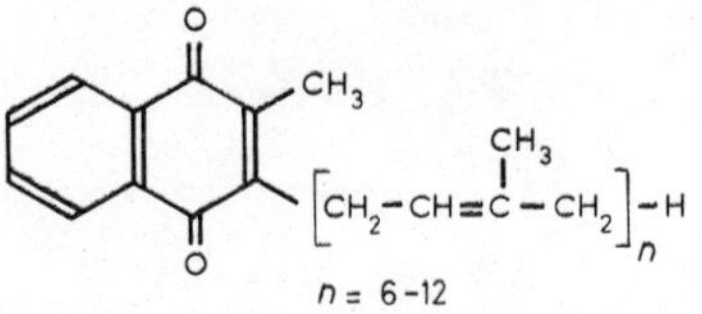

$$\text{Menaquinone: 2-methyl-1,4-naphthoquinone-3-}[CH_2-CH{=}C(CH_3)-CH_2]_n-H, \quad n = 6\text{–}12$$

Fig. 2.20 The structure of menaquinone.

by the replacement of one carrier by another with essentially similar properties, or by the deletion of one or more carriers. A good example of the former is the replacement of ubiquinone by *menaquinone* (MK; Fig. 2.20) in most Gram positive organisms, although a few Gram negative species contain both MK and Q; both quinones are lipophilic hydrogen carriers, albeit of rather different redox potential (E_m MK/MKH$_2$ = -74 mV, cf. $\leq +150$ mV) and they serve essentially the same function in the respiratory chain. Similarly, cytochrome oxidase aa_3 is often replaced by cytochrome oxidase a_1 (which contains two haems a, E_m + 160 and + 260 mV, and is a close structural relative of aa_3), o (which contains two protohaems, E_m variable in the range -120 to $+147$ mV) or d (originally called a_2; Section 2.5), or by various combinations of these oxidases. Finally, in a few species of bacteria the energy-linked transhydrogenase is replaced by an energy-independent enzyme which is either soluble or membrane-bound. Deletions are usually restricted to transhydrogenase and cytochrome c; a large number of different organisms contain respiratory chains which are deficient in one or both of these components.

On the basis of their redox carrier compositions and their sensitivities to classical inhibitors of mitochondrial respiration, the aerobic respiratory chains of bacteria may loosely be divided into two groups, viz. those which, at least superficially, resemble mitochondrial systems, and those which exhibit much greater diversity and are uniquely bacterial. The respiratory chains of *Paracoccus denitrificans*, *Alcaligenes eutrophus* and many Gram positive bacteria fall into the first category (Fig. 2.21a); indeed, a somewhat tenuous hypothesis has been proposed that mitochondria may have evolved as the result of endosymbiosis involving an ancestral form of *Pc. denitrificans* and a primitive host cell. Into the second category fall the respiratory chains of most, but not all, Gram negative chemoheterotrophs, including *Escherichia coli*, *Azotobacter vinelandii* and many species of *Pseudomonas* (Fig. 2.21b). It should be noted that bacterial respiratory chains, like those of mitochondria, contain multiple Fe–S proteins, and *b*- and *c*-type cytochromes; as is clearly evident, however, they are much more diverse than their

(a) (NADPH →) NADH → FMN·Fe-S → MK (or Q) → b → c → (aa_3 or o)

(b) (NADPH →) NADH → FMN·Fe-S → Q (and MK) → b → (c) → (a_1 d or o)

Fig. 2.21 The aerobic respiratory chains of chemoheterotrophic bacteria (brackets indicate the sites of potential replacements or deletions).

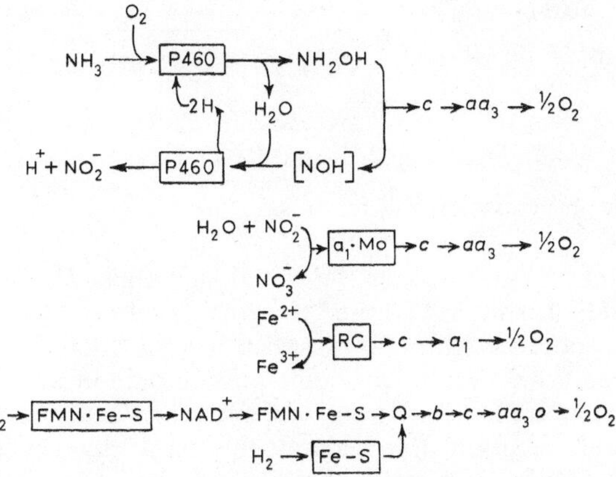

Fig. 2.22 The aerobic respiratory chains of chemolithotrophic bacteria.

mitochondrial counterparts. Furthermore, since bacteria, unlike mitochondria, live an independent existence in a potentially changing environment, their respiratory chains often alter significantly as a function of the growth conditions. For example, a typical response to low oxygen tensions is to increase the cytochrome oxidase concentration, and perhaps also the number of different oxidases, in order to enable the cell to compete as effectively as possible for the limited supply of oxidant.

Several species of bacteria are known in which the essentially linear sequence of redox carriers is branched at the level of the *b*- or *c*-type cytochromes. A prime example of this is the respiratory chain of the obligate aerobe *Az. vinelandii* in which the two branches can be used differentially as part of a mechanism to protect the nitrogen-fixation system of the organism from the potentially deleterious effects of excess oxygen.

The respiratory chains of chemolithotropic bacteria show a number of interesting variations on those of aerobic chemoheterotrophs, notably the presence of novel redox carriers which catalyse the initial oxidation of the inorganic electron donors (Fig. 2.22). Thus, for example, the oxidation of ammonia by *Nitrosomonas* is initiated by its oxygenation to hydroxylamine via cytochrome P460, a specialized *b*-type cytochrome; this reaction decreases the $E'_{\ominus}$ of the reducing couple from + 899 mV (hydroxylamine/ammonia) to + 66 mV (nitrite/hydroxylamine) and thus enables significant energy conservation to occur during aerobic respiration; the subsequent oxidation of hydroxylamine generates nitroxyl, which is stabilized by its P460-dependent conversion to nitrite. The oxidation of nitrite ($E'_{\ominus}$ nitrate/nitrite = + 420 mV) by *Nitrobacter* involves a specialized cytochrome $a_1 \cdot$ molybdoprotein system, and the oxidation of Fe^{2+} ($E'_{\ominus}$ Fe^{3+}/Fe^{2+} = + 780 mV) by *Thiobacillus ferrooxidans* occurs via a copper protein, rusticyanin. The oxidation of reduced sulphur compounds (e.g. S^{2-}, $S_2O_3^{2-}$ and SO_3^{2-}) by *Thiobacillus* and *Sulfolobus* is complex and is outside the scope of this book; there is

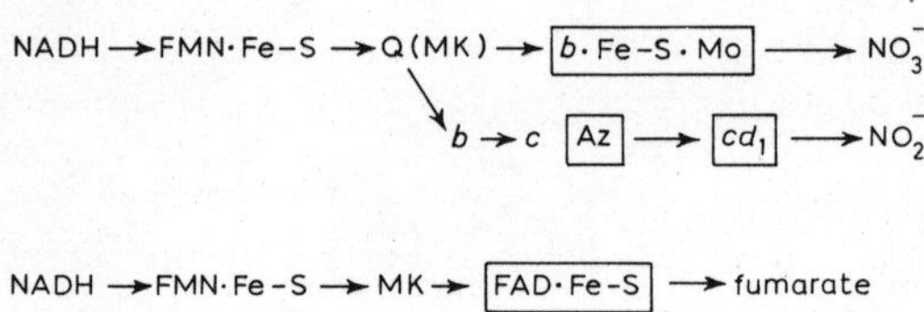

Fig. 2.23 Anaerobic respiratory chains.

some evidence, however, that the initial steps may also involve novel redox carriers. It should be noted that the oxidation of these relatively high redox potential inorganic substrates is often independent of flavoproteins, iron–sulphur proteins and/or quinones, although these carriers are required for the energy-dependent reversal of respiration via which these chemolithotrophs generate the NAD(P)H which they require for carbon dioxide assimilation (Section 4.6). In contrast, the oxidation of hydrogen ($E'_{\ominus}$ $2H^+/H_2 = -420\,mV$) by diverse Gram negative bacteria, including the facultative chemolithotrophs *Pc·denitrificans* and *Alc·eutrophus*, occurs either via a soluble NAD^+-linked hydrogenase which contains FMN and several types of Fe–S centres, or via a membrane-bound enzyme which lacks the flavin and donates electrons to ubiquinone/cytochrome *b*; only in this latter case is reversed electron transfer required for NAD(P)H generation.

Anaerobic respiratory chains also show significant differences from those which catalyse aerobic respiration, notably the presence of appropriate reductases, many of which contain novel redox carriers (Fig. 2.23). Thus the dissimilatory reduction of nitrate in *E. coli* and many denitrifying bacteria, including *Pc. denitrificans*, occurs via a nitrate reductase which contains a specialized *b*-type cytochrome and Fe–S/Mo proteins. The reduction by denitrifying bacteria of the resultant nitrite to nitrogen, probably via NO and N_2O, involves a copper protein, azurin, and a specialized dihaem protein, cytochrome cd_1 (nitrite reductase). The dissimilatory reduction of various oxidized sulphur compounds (e.g. SO_4^{2-}, SO_3^{2-}) by *Desulfovibrio* and *Desulfotomaculum*, and of carbon dioxide by various methanogenic bacteria, both involve a number of novel redox carriers, but these reactions are too complicated to be considered here. On the other hand, the widespread reduction of fumarate to succinate is a fairly simple process and is catalysed by an MK-linked enzyme, fumarate reductase, which contains no novel redox carriers and is strikingly similar to succinate dehydrogenase. Since most of these organic and inorganic oxidants are of relatively low redox potential compared with oxygen, the respiratory chains which catalyse their reduction are often deficient in *b*- and/or *c*-type cytochromes, and cytochrome oxidases.

This latter observation emphasizes the dynamic nature of bacterial respiratory chains compared with those of mitochondria. Thus although both *E. coli* and *Pc. denitrificans*, for example, can utilize a wide range of electron donors and acceptors, they synthesize relatively few redox carriers constitutively; the synthesis of the majority is subject to induction or repression by the available reductant and/or oxidant such that energy and resources are not wasted on the formation of unnecessary respiratory chain components.

Finally, it should be noted that in addition to the classical procedures described earlier in this chapter for determining redox carrier sequences in mitochondria, bacterial respiratory chains can be investigated via genotypic and phenotypic manipulation. The former approach has been applied with great success to the facultative anaerobe *E. coli* by Gibson and his colleagues who have shown, for example, that ubiquinone-deficient (Ubi^-) or protohaem-deficient (Hem^-) mutants of this organism will grow anaerobically on glucose, but not aerobically on a non-fermentable carbon source, thus indicating that ubiquinone and *b*-type cytochromes are essential components of the respiratory chain. Similarly, Garland and his colleagues have shown that cultures of *E. coli* grown in media which are deficient in iron, sulphate, molybdenum or selenium exhibit lesions in energy coupling, nitrate reduction and formate oxidation respectively, thus confirming a role for Fe–S proteins, molybdoproteins and/or selenoproteins in these processes. These two techniques are currently being applied to other species of bacteria and to other redox components.

2.9 Electron and hydrogen transfer

Williams has pointed out that the presence of metal (Fe, Cu, Mo) and non-metal (nicotinamide, flavin, quinone) redox centres may be of great significance to respiratory chain function [14]. The metals are associated with electron transfer and with oxygen atom transfer; only rarely are they associated with the transfer of hydrogen atoms. Iron, being a transition element, can exist readily in several oxidation states and hence can operate over a wide range of redox potential (compare Fe–S centre N–1a with cytochrome a_3). It is therefore the ideal metal for a respiratory system since it can effectively bridge the entire redox potential span, and can react with oxygen and various inorganic donors and acceptors; since the iron–protein redox carriers exhibit low activation energies, electron transfer between them is energetically relatively easy and is of specified direction. Many of these properties are also shared by copper and molybdenum. Conversely, the individual organic redox centres are of relatively fixed redox potential and are generally concerned with the transfer of hydrogen atoms or hydride ions, both of which occur relatively slowly. The nicotinamide nucleotides and flavins react most easily with activated hydrogen (e.g. the —CHOH of lactate and malate, the $—CH_2{\cdot}CH_2{\cdot}CO—$ of succinate and fatty acyl CoA, and the —CH=CH— of fumarate), but not with oxygen or other inorganic donors and acceptors.

The presence of separate clusters of these two types of redox carriers has important implications for respiratory chain energy conservation. Firstly they allow rapid respiration to occur, since the redox potentials of adjacent carriers are fairly well matched. Secondly, respiration can be accompanied by the ejection or uptake of protons at metal/non-metal junctions, a phenomenon which may be crucial to the mechanism of energy transduction (Chapter 5).

3 The organization and function of the coupling membrane

We have seen in the previous chapter that the redox reactions which comprise respiration occur in a strictly defined sequence. In this respect they resemble the multienzyme pathways of glycolysis, the tricarboxylic acid cycle and the fatty acid oxidation spiral. However, in contrast to these latter processes, respiration and oxidative phosphorylation are completely membrane-bound, being located in the mitochondrial inner membrane of eukaryotic cells and in the cytoplasmic membrane of bacteria. Since these membranes couple respiration to ATP synthesis (and other energy-utilizing reactions), they are often referred to as *coupling membranes*.

Clearly, the major function of these membranes is to organize the individual redox carriers, the respiratory chain complexes and the ATP-synthesizing apparatus into an efficient and easily regulated energy-transducing unit. In addition, the coupling membrane plays an intrinsic role in the mechanism of energy transduction itself, since the latter cannot occur in the absence of a membrane structure and is seriously impaired if the integrity of the membrane is damaged (see Chapters 4 and 5). Finally, the coupling membrane is one of the major permeability barriers of the cell, particularly in bacteria, since it strictly controls the movement of a wide range of solutes into and out of the compartment which it encloses. The membrane therefore grossly controls its own respiratory activity by regulating the supply of some essential substrates and cofactors, and at the same time protects itself from the deleterious effects of osmotic imbalance. These functions, which are common to all coupling membranes, have been intensively investigated in mitochondria and, to a lesser extent, in various species of bacteria.

3.1 Mitochondrial structure and function

The mitochondria are the sites of respiration and oxidative phosphorylation in all animal and higher plant tissues, as well as in protozoa, fungi and aerobically grown yeasts. In the former they are usually found in abundance where ATP requirements for biosynthetic, secretory or mechanochemical activities are greatest (e.g. liver, pancreas, muscle) or

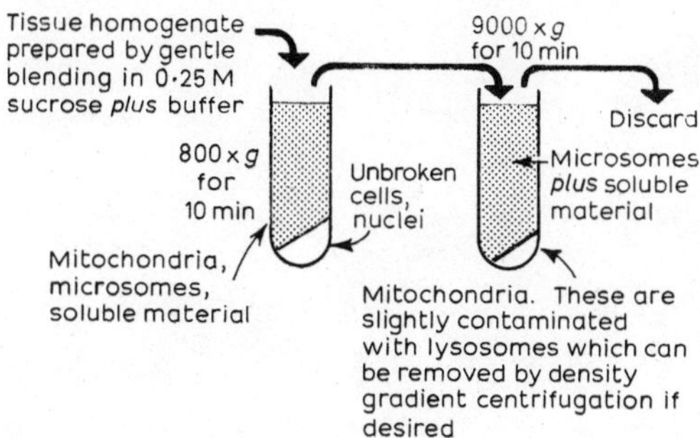

Fig. 3.1 The isolation of intact mitochondria.

where the supply of oxidizable substrates is most prolific (e.g. brain, adipose tissue).

Although mitochondria were first observed microscopically in the mid-nineteenth century, it was not until 1947 that Pallade and co-workers successfully isolated these organelles intact [15]. The trick was to disrupt the tissue gently in an isotonic solution of buffered sucrose at 0–4°C, thus preventing osmotic lysis of these relatively fragile organelles. The homogenate was then subjected to differential centrifugation in order to separate the mitochondria from unbroken cells, nuclei, microsomes and soluble material. This technique has since been slightly refined (Fig. 3.1) and can be used for the isolation of large quantities of mitochondria which are competent in both respiration and a variety of energy-linked functions.

Mitochondria vary in shape and size quite markedly according to their origin (hence their name, derived from the Greek, mitos = thread, *chondros* = grain); sausage-shaped mitochondria, such as those present in rat liver and beef heart, are approximately 2–3 μm long and 0.5–1 μm wide. Electron micrographs of negatively stained mitochondria in transverse section clearly show two membranes, viz. a limiting *outer membrane* and a highly invaginated *inner membrane*, the infoldings of which are called *cristae*. These membranes divide the mitochondrion into two separate compartments, viz. the space between the membranes (the *intermembrane space*) and the space which is enclosed by the inner membrane (the *matrix*) (Fig. 3.2a).

The outer membrane is 60–70 Å thick, smooth and unfolded. It is relatively inelastic, but is freely permeable to molecules of mol. wt. $\leq$ 10 000. Analysis of this membrane, which can be separated from the rest of the mitochondrion by brief exposure to the detergent digitonin or by swelling in hypotonic buffer, indicates that it has a high ratio of phospholipid to protein and that it contains a heterogeneous group of enzymes which catalyse various aspects of lipid metabolism plus several important hydroxylation reactions. In contrast, the inner membrane shows some evidence of substructure on its matrix-facing surface (Section 3.2.1.) and exhibits differential solute permeabilities. It affords

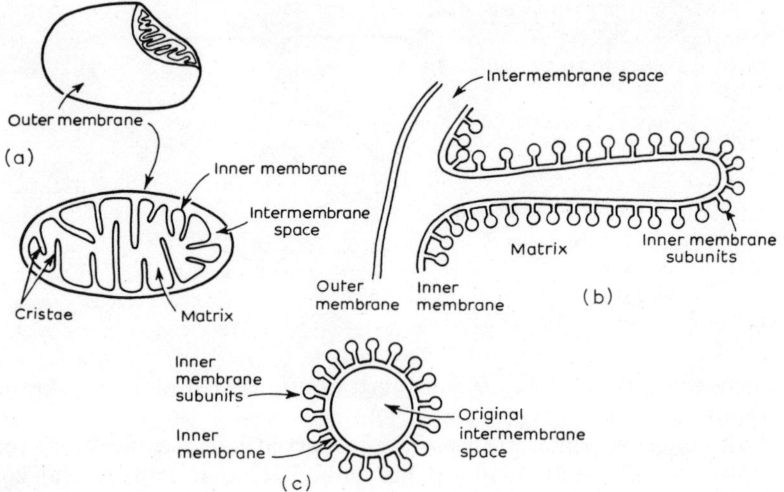

Fig. 3.2 The morphology of mitochondria and submitochondrial particles in transverse section. (a) The mitochondrion, (b) the mitochondrial inner membrane, and (c) a submitochondrial particle.

no hindrance to the diffusion of small, uncharged molecules (e.g. water, oxygen, carbon dioxide, ammonia, ethanol), but its permeability to hydrophilic ions (e.g. nicotinamide and adenine nucleotides, phosphate, H^+) is extremely limited except via the mediation of specific transport systems. Thus it is the inner membrane, rather than the relatively porous outer membrane, which is the major permeability barrier between the cytoplasm and the matrix. This 60–80 Å thick membrane has a low phospholipid to protein ratio, and offers a very large surface area by virtue of its highly invaginated nature; it houses the respiratory chain, the ATP-synthesizing apparatus and a variety of solute carriers. The intermembrane space is 60–80 Å wide and contains very few enzymes, most of which catalyse the interconversion of adenine nucleotides (e.g. nucleoside diphosphate kinase and adenylate kinase). The matrix, on the other hand, is extremely viscous and contains the vast array of enzymes that comprise the tricarboxylic acid cycle (with the exception of succinate dehydrogenase which is in the inner membrane), the fatty acid oxidation spiral and part of the urea cycle, together with those that catalyse the synthesis of mitochondrial DNA and RNA. It is these first two amphibolic and catabolic pathways of intermediary metabolism which provide the adjacent respiratory chain with its major oxidisable substrate, NADH.

3.2 The organization of the mitochondrial energy conservation system

It is necessary now to examine the properties of the enzyme complex which catalyses the synthesis of ATP at the expense of redox energy, to consider the organization of the respiratory chain within the coupling membrane, and to see how these two processes are functionally and morphologically related.

3.2.1 *The morphology and properties of the ATP phosphohydrolase complex*

In 1964 Fernandez-Moran reported the presence of repeating structures on the inner membranes of negatively stained mitochondria [16]. These structures were present on the side of the membrane which faced the matrix (*M-side*), but they were totally absent from the side which faced the cytoplasm (*C-side*) and also from either side of the outer membrane. High magnification electron micrographs showed that each of these structures consisted of a roughly spherical *head piece* or *inner membrane sphere* (80–100 Å diameter) which was attached to a membrane portion via a *stalk* (40–50 Å long) (Fig. 3.2b). However, it is possible that the stalks are embedded into the membrane *in vivo*, such that the headpieces lie on the surface of the membrane rather protrude into the matrix.

When intact mitochondria are subjected to ultrasonication they disintegrate and the inner membrane fragments reform into vesicles which are called *submitochondrial particles*. Electron micrographs of the latter indicate that the headpieces are now located on the outside surface of the vesicles; the inside surface is smooth (Fig. 3.2c). Submitochondrial particles are thus considered to be 'inside-out', relative to the inner membrane of the parent mitochondria. In spite of this, when prepared carefully they retain their ability to couple respiration to ATP synthesis with fairly high efficiency.

Using submitochondrial particles, Racker was able to demonstrate that removal of the headpieces by mechanical treatment yielded a soluble enzyme complex (F_1) which exhibited considerable ATP-hydrolysing (*ATPase*) activity. The depleted membranes no longer showed any ATP-synthesizing (*ATP synthetase*) activity, although they were still capable of respiration. When F_1 was added back to the membranes under carefully controlled conditions, the latter again took on the appearance of submitochondrial particles and exhibited oxidative phosphorylation. These elegant experiments thus demonstrated that the repeating structures on the inner membrane house the reversible *ATP phosphohydrolase* (*ATPase-ATP synthetase*) *complex* or *Complex V* which is responsible for transducing the redox energy of the respiratory chain into the hydrolysis energy of ATP [17, 18].

It is now known that the ATP phosphohydrolase complex (mol. wt. ≅ 500 000) is comprised of F_1 (an assembly of hydrophilic peptides) and F_0 (a membrane-bound complex of hydrophobic peptides and proteolipids). It contains at least 11 different peptides and catalyses three major activities, viz., ATP hydrolysis, ATP-Pi exchange and ATP synthesis, at the expense of energy released during respiration. All three reactions are inhibited by a variety of reagents, including the antibiotics oligomycin and aurovertin, and the functional-group reagents 4-chloro-

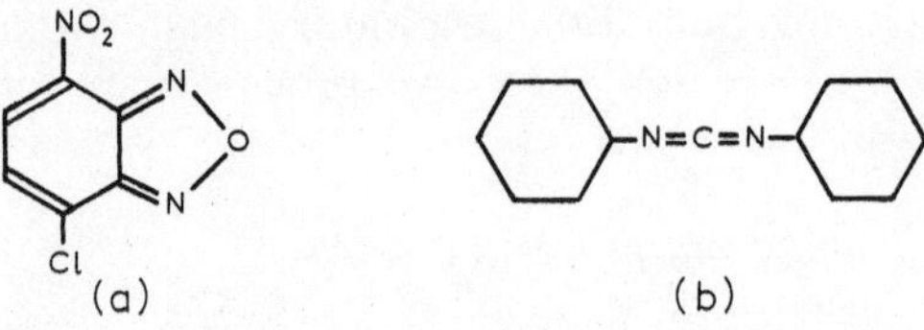

Fig. 3.3 Inhibitors of the ATP phosphohydrolase complex. (a) Nbf–Cl, and (b) DCCD.

7-nitrobenzofurazan (Nbf-Cl) and *N,N'-dicyclohexylcarbodiimide* (DCCD) (Fig. 3.3).

The role of F_1 (mol. wt. 350 000) in the ATP phosphohydrolase complex is primarily catalytic. It is comprised of five different subunits in the approximate ratio $\alpha_3\beta_3\gamma\delta\varepsilon$. The α and β subunits are responsible for binding one molecule of Mg^{2+} and for the presence of six adenine nucleotide binding sites; four of these contain tightly bound nucleotides (2ATP, 2ADP) and probably have a regulatory function, whereas the other two reversibly bind exogenous nucleotides and are probably responsible for the catalytic activity of F_1. The minor subunits have structural and/or regulatory functions. A sixth subunit (I), which may or may not remain attached to the β subunit depending on the purification procedure employed, is a potent inhibitor of ATPase activity and hence may function *in vivo* to minimize the wasteful hydrolysis of ATP (an activity which is usually latent in intact mitochondria). The ATPase activity of isolated F_1 is inhibited by aurovertin and Nbf-Cl (both of which bind to the β subunit), but not by oligomycin or DCCD; in addition, F_1 exhibits the relatively unusual property of cold lability, although the latter is lost when F_1 is bound to the membrane. These phenomena, whereby enzymes exhibit modified properties when separated from the membrane, are examples of *allotopy*.

Unlike F_1, F_0 has no obvious enzyme activity. It consists of at least five subunits, viz. the oligomycin-sensitivity conferring protein (OSCP), the DCCD-binding protein (DCCD-BP, which probably also binds oligomycin), the uncoupler binding protein (UBP), F_6 and F_2 (also called factor B). F_0 is attached to F_1 via OSCP, in association with F_6;

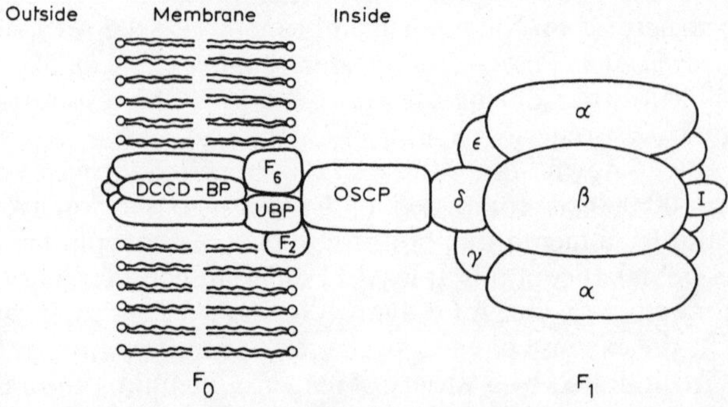

Fig. 3.4 The structure of the ATP phosphohydrolase complex.

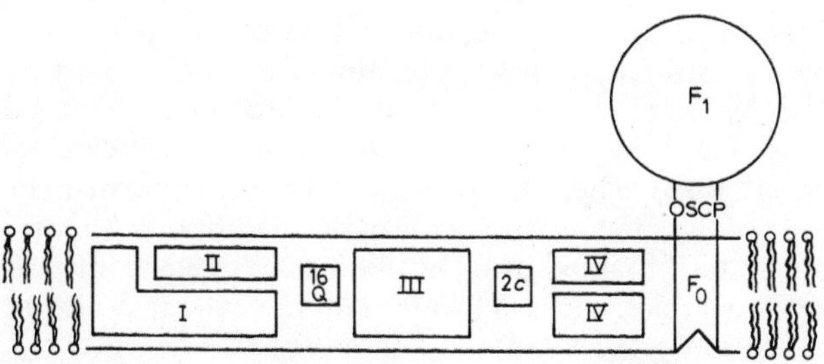

Fig. 3.5 Diagrammatic representation of a respiratory chain energy conservation unit (after Slater, 1972).

OSCP and/or F_6 thus probably form the stalk of the ATP phosphohydrolase complex (Fig. 3.4). The function of the DCCD-binding protein, which probably aggregates into a hexamer *in vivo*, is to form an H^+-translocating channel through F_0 and thus (in association with UBP, F_2, F_6, OSCP and the $\gamma, \delta, \varepsilon$ subunits) to allow the transmembrane movement of H^+ to and from the active site(s) of F_1 (see Section 5.2.3).

The inner membrane contains approximately one antimycin-binding site (complex III) and one oligomycin-binding site (F_0) per molecule of F_1. Thus, since each respiratory chain unit contains only one molecule of complex III, the energy released by respiration is harnessed by a single molecule of the ATP phosphohydrolase complex (Fig. 3.5).

3.2.2 *The asymmetric organization of respiratory chain components*

The intramembrane organization of the respiratory chain complexes I–IV, and their constituent redox carriers, is a particularly difficult problem to investigate since, unlike complex V, they rarely protrude significantly from the surface of the membrane and hence cannot be directly visualized by electron microscopy. The problem has thus been tackled principally through the use of selected agents which do not penetrate the membrane and which therefore interact with the predominantly hydrophilic carriers that are located close to the surface (*extrinsic components*), but not with the more hydrophobic carriers which are deeply embedded in the phospholipid bilayer (*intrinsic components*) [4–9, 19]. These agents include reductants (NADH, NADPH, ferrocytochrome *c*, ferrocyanide), oxidants (ferricytochrome *c*, ferricyanide), inhibitors (antibodies, hydrophilic chelating agents), protein-labelling reagents (diazobenzene-[^{35}S]-sulphonate, [$Na^{125}I$] plus lactoperoxidase) and membrane-extracting reagents (proteases, phospholipases, silicotungstate). When added to intact mitochondria these molecules react with redox carriers which are located on the cytoplasmic side (*C-side*) of the membrane, but not with those which are located on the matrix side (*M-side*); the converse is true with submitochondrial particles where the polarity of the membrane is reversed. Thus, for example, Racker showed in a series of classical experiments that antibodies to cytochrome *c* (the most easily purified redox carrier and hence the easiest to use for antibody production) readily inhibited the respiration of intact mitochondria (the outer membrane is freely permeable to antibodies), but not of submitochondrial particles. However, when the latter were prepared in the presence of antibodies such that they became trapped within the lumen of the particles, respiration was again inhibited. These experiments therefore indicated clearly that cytochrome *c* is located on the C-side of the membrane. Almost identical results were later obtained using antibodies to cytochrome c_1, whereas antibodies to F_1 confirmed its location on the M-side of the membrane as previously indicated by electron microscopy.

Using the various methods outlined above, it has been shown that transhydrogenase probably bridges the membrane; its substrate-binding sites, like those of complexes I and II, are located on the M-side (i.e. in close contact with the enzymes of the tricarboxylic acid cycle and the fatty acid oxidation spiral which supply the substrates). Complex I contains some subunits which are transmembranous and others which are restricted to the C-side, interior or M-side of the membrane; the flavoprotein is situated close to the M-side, whereas the iron–sulphur proteins either span the membrane or are buried within it. There is some evidence that although complex II also physically spans the membrane, its redox components (and hence its electron transfer functions) are restricted to the M-side. Complexes I and II both donate reducing equivalents to the protein-bound ubiquinone pair which is located close to the M-side; the remainder of the ubiquinone appears to occupy a transmembrane location. Complex III also appears to span the membrane, the iron–sulphur protein being located close to cytochrome *c* on the C-side, and the *b*-type cytochromes occypying positions which range across to the M-side. The location of complex IV was initially the subject of considerable controversy since the results of histochemical in-

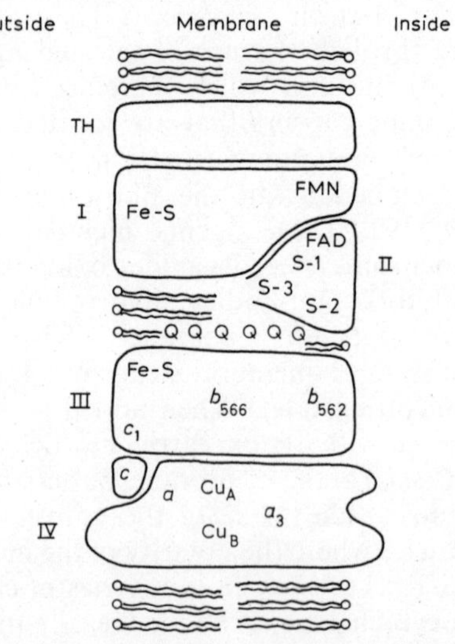

Fig. 3.6 The organization of the mitochondrial respiratory chain.

vestigations assigned it to the C-side, whereas the ability of azide to inhibit mitochondrial respiration most effectively under conditions where it was accumulated suggested a location on the M-side. It is now known that the enzyme bridges the membrane, and indeed protrudes slightly on either side; cytochrome *a* is close to cytochrome *c* on the C-side, whereas the two copper atoms and cytochrome a_3 are in the centre/M-side. The final step of respiration is, therefore, the inward transfer of electrons through cytochrome oxidase from the C-side to the M-side of the membrane (Fig. 3.6). Interestingly, complexes I, II and III each contain at least one extremely hydrophobic subunit which is deeply embedded in the membrane and, like the DCCD-binding proteolipid of complex V, could possibly function as an ion-translocating channel (see Section 5.4).

3.3 Mitochondrial solute transport

The ability of the coupling membrane to translocate various solutes will only be discussed where these solutes are of immediate importance to energy transduction (e.g. oxygen, NADH, succinate, adenine nucleotides, inorganic phosphate and H^+). It should be noted, however, that the transport of other solutes (e.g. citrate, malate, glutamate, aspartate) is essential to the compartmented provision of carbon skeletons and ammonia for the synthesis of glucose, fatty acids and urea [20]. The coupling membrane presents no barrier to the movement of dissolved oxygen or its respiratory product, water. Furthermore, NADH and succinate are both produced in the matrix and therefore have free access to the active sites of their respective dehydrogenases; in contrast, NADH generated in the cytoplasm during glycolysis must be imported across the membrane (although some plant and yeast mitochondria avoid this problem by having a second, rotenone-insensitive NADH dehydrogenase with its substrate-binding site on the C-side of the membrane). Since the latter is impermeable to NAD(P)H and $NAD(P)^+$, translocation of reducing equivalents must occur indirectly via metabolite shuttles such as the *Borst cycle* and the *glycerol-3-phosphate shuttle* (Fig. 3.7a, b). The former is a complex series of reactions which involves malate dehydrogenase, aspartate amino transferase and two membrane-

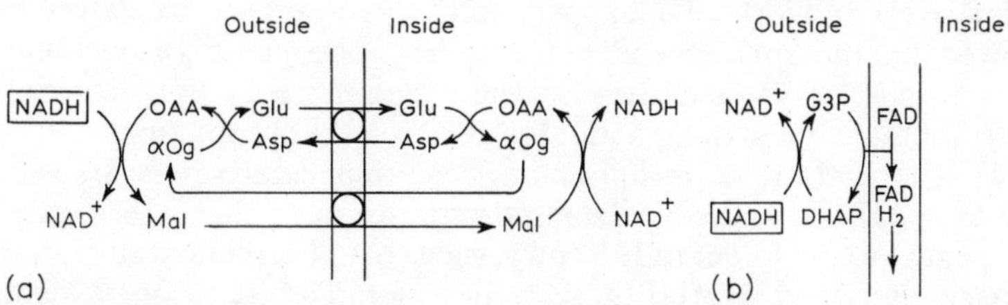

Fig. 3.7 The transport of reducing equivalents across the mitochondrial inner membrane. (a) the Borst cycle, and (b) the glycerol-3-phosphate shuttle. Abbreviations: OAA, oxaloacetate; αOg, α-oxoglutarate; glu, glutamate; asp, aspartate; mal, malate; G3P, glycerol-3-phosphate; DHAP, dihydroxyacetone phosphate.

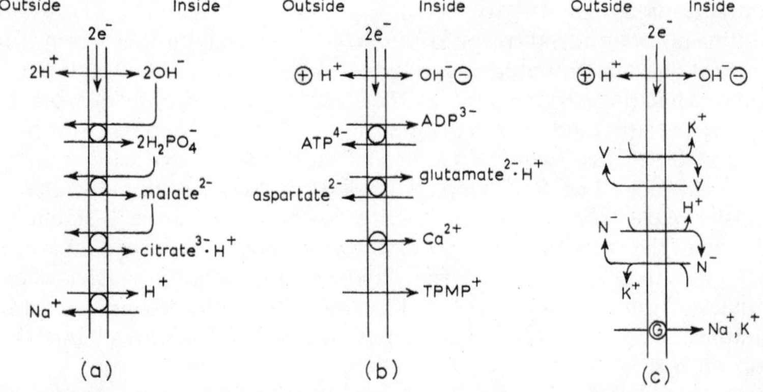

Fig. 3.8 The transport of ions across the mitochondrial inner membrane. (a) ΔpH-dependent, (b) $\Delta\psi$-dependent, and (c) ionophore-mediated. Abbreviations: V, valinomycin; N, nigericin; G, gramicidin.

bound solute carriers, and which catalyses the unidirectional influx of NADH into most types of mammalian mitochondria. In contrast, the glycerol-3-phosphate shuttle is mainly associated with insect mitochondria, and involves NAD^+- and FAD-linked glycerol-3-phosphate dehydrogenases which are located in the cytoplasm and on the C-side of the membrane, respectively; the shuttle thus generates $FADH_2$ at the expense of NADH, with an attendant loss of ATP-synthesizing efficiency.

There is now considerable evidence that respiration, either directly or indirectly, generates a transmembrane *electrochemical potential difference of H^+* (the *protonmotive force*, Δp or $\Delta\,\bar{\mu}H^+$), which is comprised of an *osmotic* or *chemical potential difference* (ΔpH; pH_{out} minus pH_{in}) and an *electrical potential difference* or *membrane potential* ($\Delta\psi$; Section 5.2.1). As a result, the matrix of the mitochondrion becomes alkaline and electrically negative relative to the intermembrane space and the surrounding cytoplasm. The *accumulative transport* (*active transport*) of charged molecules through the coupling membrane is therefore driven by ΔpH and/or $\Delta\psi$ depending on the precise nature of the transported species.

The elegant work of Chappell and co-workers in the late 1960s showed that the ΔpH-dependent transport of phosphate is a key event in the transport of di- and tricarboxylates (Fig. 3.8a). $H_2PO_4^-$ enters the matrix compartment in exchange for OH^- via the phosphate carrier; the latter, a typical *exchange-diffusion system*, thus catalyses *electroneutral* $H_2PO_4^- \cdot OH^-$ *antiport* (it is important to note that OH^- exit is energetically equivalent to H^+ entry, such that phosphate transport can also be described as $H_2PO_4^- \cdot H^+$ *symport*). This reaction is readily inhibited by a variety of -SH group reagents, including *N*-ethylmaleimide (NEM). The movement of phosphate is the primary event of a 'cascade' process in which the subsequent exit of this anion drives the uptake of malate and other dicarboxylates (via the dicarboxylate carrier), and the subsequent exit of malate is linked to the uptake of citrate and isocitrate (via the tricarboxylate carrier) and of α-oxoglutarate (via the α-oxoglutarate carrier).

The transport of ATP and ADP, but not AMP, via the adenine nucleotide translocase (Fig. 3.8b) reflects the different adenine nucleotide requirements of the matrix (low [ATP]/[ADP] ratio for oxidative phosphorylation) and the cytoplasm (high [ATP]/[ADP] ratio for biosynthesis). There is extensive evidence from Klingenberg's laboratory [21] that the export of ATP^{4-} is obligatorily linked to the uptake of ADP^{3-} and, since the two nucleotides are of unequal charge, that the adenine nucleotide translocase catalyses *electrogenic* antiport under the driving force of the $\Delta\psi$; the latter greatly enhances the rates of ATP exit and ADP entry compared with de-energized conditions. The asymmetry of adenine nucleotide transport is also reflected in its sensitivity to specific inhibitors, in that carboxyatractyloside (CAT) and bongkrekate (BKA) inhibit most effectively from the C-side and the M-side of the membrane, respectively. The adenine nucleotide translocase is comprised of two identical hydrophobic peptides (mol. wt. 2 × 30 000); since two molecules of translocase are present per respiratory chain unit, it is easily the most abundant protein in the mitochondrion.

The coupling membrane is naturally relatively impermeable to H^+, K^+ and $Na^+ \cdot H^+$ drawn in by the Δp is ejected via respiration, and excess Na^+ drawn in by the $\Delta\psi$ is ejected via an $Na^+ \cdot H^+$ antiporter; the latter thus maintains the high $[Na^+]_{out}/[Na^+]_{in}$ ratio which is characteristic of intact mitochondria. The permeability of the coupling membrane to these cations can be increased by the addition of *mobile* or *channel-forming ionophores*, including the lipophilic antibiotics *valinomycin* (K^+ uniport), *nigericin* ($K^+ \cdot H^+$ antiport) and *gramicidin* (K^+ or Na^+ uniport; Fig. 3.8c); a number of ionophores are also known which are specific to H^+ (Section 4.4). In contrast to monovalent cations, Ca^{2+} (and to a lesser extent Mn^{2+}, Sr^{2+} and Mg^{2+}) are rapidly accumulated in the matrix during respiration; uptake occurs principally via a high affinity Ca^{2+} carrier which catalyses electrogenic uniport at the expense of $\Delta\psi$, and is specifically inhibited by ruthenium red and lanthanum ion (La^{3+}). Ca^{2+} efflux probably occurs via $\Delta\psi$-independent, $Ca^{2+} \cdot 2H^+$ and $Ca^{2+} \cdot 2Na^+$ antiport. The relative rates of Ca^{2+} uptake and efflux determine the concentration of Ca^{2+} in the cytoplasm and matrix, and hence control the activities of various Ca^{2+}-dependent enzymes in these two compartments [22].

3.4 The morphology and organization of the bacterial coupling membrane

The cytoplasmic membrane, which is the site of energy coupling in bacteria, is normally located in the cell envelope, although in some chemolithotrophs and specialized chemoheterotrophs it invades the cytoplasm in the form of deep invaginations or concentric layers. It is the only membrane in Gram positive organisms, but in Gram negative bacteria it is surrounded by an *outer membrane* from which it is separated by the *periplasmic space*. Under the appropriate conditions, the enzyme lysozyme will dissolve away the cell wall of both types of cells to leave, in isotonic media, intact *protoplasts* and *sphaeroplasts*, respectively. Mechanical disruption of these structures (or the original whole cells) produces relatively small, *inside-out membrane vesicles* which are analogous to submitochondrial particles and, like the latter, have been extensively used for studying oxidative phosphorylation. In contrast, their exposure to osmotic shock yields relatively large, *right-side-out membrane vesicles* which are particularly suitable for investigating solute transport.

The bacterial ATP phosphohydrolase complex, particularly from *E. coli* and the thermophile PS3, has been extensively analysed using physico-chemical and genetic techniques. Like that of mitochondria, it is comprised of two peptide assemblies (BF_0 and BF_1) and is asymmetrically located in the coupling membrane. BF_1 faces the cytoplasm, which is equivalent to the matrix compartment in mitochondria, and is similar to F_1 except that it appears to lack a separate ATPase-inhibitor peptide; the role of the latter is taken over by the ε-subunit. BF_0, which spans the coupling membrane, has similar properties to F_0 but is probably comprised of fewer peptides and is usually insensitive to oligomycin. $BF_0 \cdot BF_1$ functions predominantly as an ATP synthetase in respiratory bacteria, but in fermentative organisms it serves only to hydrolyse ATP formed by substrate-level phosphorylation (Section 4.7).

Surprisingly little is known about the organization of bacterial respiratory chains, although the recent work of Garland and his colleagues on relatively simple anaerobic and chemolithotrophic sys-

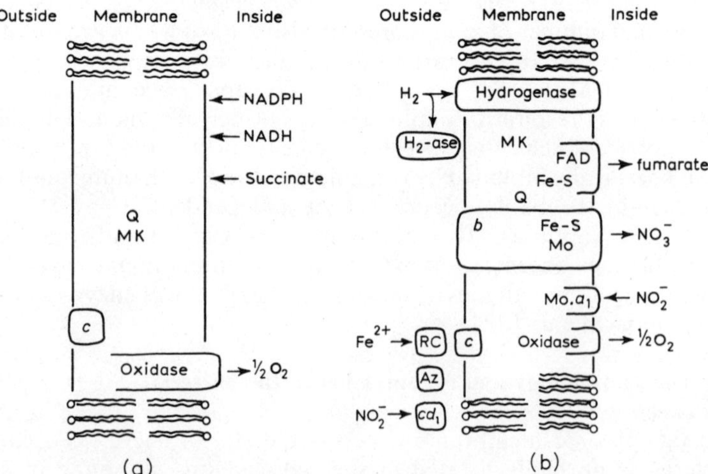

Fig. 3.9 The organization of bacterial respiratory chains in (a) aerobic chemoheterotrophs, and (b) chemolithotrophs and anaerobic chemoheterotrophs.

tems has done much to alleviate this deficiency. There is some evidence that the active sites of most dehydrogenases, oxidases and reductases are located on the inner surface of the coupling membrane; exceptions to this are rusticyanin and nitrite reductase (cytochrome cd_1), which are in the periplasmic space, and cytochrome c and the active site of hydrogenase, which are on the outer surface of the membrane. Hydrogenase and nitrate reductase have been shown to span the coupling membrane and, like mitochondrial cytochrome oxidase, to act as inwardly directed transmembrane electron carriers (Fig. 3.9).

3.5 Bacterial solute transport

The majority of bacteria are free-living organisms. They are therefore faced, even more stringently than mitochondria, with the problem of maintaining a constant internal solute composition in the presence of a potentially hostile, ever-changing environment. Since essential co-factors must not be allowed to leave the cell, bacterial coupling membranes generally lack both the adenine nucleotide translocase and the various nicotinamide nucleotide shuttle systems which are present in the inner membrane of the mitochondrion. They do, however, exhibit a wide range of transport phenomena, including free and facilitated diffusion (which allow the *non-accumulative transport* of small uncharged molecules) and active transport. Kaback, Harold, Hamilton and others have shown that the majority of physiological ions, to which the membrane is generally impermeable, and other nutrients are transported via the latter type of system, predominantly at the expense of ΔpH and/or $\Delta\psi$. Thus phosphate, various carboxylic acids and acidic amino acids enter by electroneutral anion-H^+ symport (ΔpH), whereas the entry of neutral amino acids occurs via electrogenic solute-H^+ symport (Δp). In contrast, the uptake of basic amino acids and many inorganic cations occurs via electrogenic uniport ($\Delta\psi$), and the ejection of unwanted cations such as Na^+ or Ca^{2+} is effected via H^+ antiport (ΔpH). The entry of nitrate and the exit of nitrite during anaerobic respiration is an intriguing problem; it seems likely that they occur via $NO_3^-{\cdot}H^+$ symport and $NO_2^-{\cdot}H^+$ antiport, respectively, the two processes combining to form an effective, Δp-driven NO_3^--NO_2^- antiport.

Active transport can also occur at the expense of driving forces other than ΔpH and/or $\Delta\psi$. Thus the uptake of glucose and certain other sugars by facultative and obligate anaerobes is catalysed by the PEP-dependent *phosphotransferase system*, and the uptake of selected amino acids can be directly powered by ATP hydrolysis. Furthermore, there is increasing evidence that some species of bacteria, particularly those like *Halobacterium halobium* which prefer high-salt environments (*halophiles*), can use an Na^+ gradient to drive solute transport; in this respect they resemble the epithelial cells of the mammalian kidney and small intestine.

Interestingly, fermentative bacteria are able to make use of the essentially reversible nature of solute transport to supplement their energy supply. *Streptococcus*, for example, generates Δp via the ejection of protons in co-transport with a metabolic end-product, lactate (i.e. via lactate·H^+ symport).

Finally, it should be noted that a variety of non-physiological lipophilic cations can be transported across bacterial (and mitochondrial) coupling membranes, without the mediation of endogenous carriers or added ionophores (e.g. [^{3}H]-triphenylmethyl phosphonium; $TPMP^+$). Like $^{42}K^+$ or $^{86}Rb^+$ in the presence of valinomycin, they rapidly distribute across the membrane in response to $\Delta\psi$ according to the Nernst equation:

$$\Delta\psi = \frac{2.303\,RT}{nF}\log\frac{[C^+]_{in}}{[C^+]_{out}}$$

where R, T and F have their usual meanings and n is the charge on the cation. $\Delta\psi$ can be accurately determined by measuring the $[C^+]_{in}/[C^+]_{out}$ ratio. ΔpH can be quantitated in a more complex manner by measuring the distribution of a permeant weak acid (e.g. [^{14}C]-5, 5-dimethyl-2, 4-oxazolidenedione; DMO). In inside-out bacterial membrane vesicles (and submitochondrial particles), where Δp is inverted compared with the parent structures, i.e. the lumen is acidic and electrically positive, $\Delta\psi$ and ΔpH can be determined by measuring the distribution of a lipophilic anion (e.g. [^{14}C]-SCN^-) and a permeant weak base (e.g. [^{14}C]-methylamine), respectively.

4 Energy coupling

The ability of crude homogenates of animal tissues to catalyse oxidative phosphorylation with endogenous or added substrates was first reported by Kalckar in 1937. It later became apparent that the amount of phosphate esterified or ATP formed was stoichiometric with the amount of oxygen consumed. This stoichiometry is called the *P/O quotient* (or *ATP/O quotient*; mol. phosphate or ATP·g-atom O^{-1}); its value reflects several parameters including the nature of the substrate undergoing oxidation, the integrity of the coupling membrane and the redox carrier composition of the respiratory chain. In the 1940s and early 1950s, workers in several different laboratories showed that the oxidation of NAD^+-linked substrates such as 3-hydroxybutyrate or malate gave ATP/O quotients of approximately 3; similar values to these have subsequently been reported on many occasions, but there has been at least one claim that they are overestimated due to systematic experimental errors.

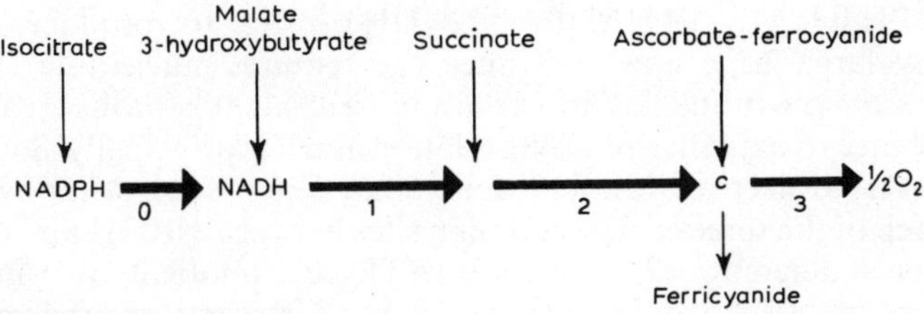

Fig. 4.1 Energy coupling sites.

A number of interesting physiological examples are known of mitochondria which exhibit abnormally low ATP/O quotients, and in which respiration is, therefore, immediately accompanied by the generation of a considerable amount of heat (*thermogenesis*); these include the mitochondria which are present in the brown adipose tissue of certain animals and in the spadices of Aroid plants. In the former example, thermogenesis ensures the survival of hibernating mammals, and combats the potentially lethal effects of cold-shock during the birth and cold adaptation of non-hibernators (Section 4.4); in the latter example it causes the evaporation of volatile oils and thus affords a means of attracting insects to assist with pollination.

4.1 Energy coupling sites

In 1954 Lehninger and Lardy independently reported the presence and location of three separate energy coupling sites in the respiratory chain of intact mitochondria. The technique which they pioneered, and which has been widely used subsequently, was to measure ATP/O ($ATP/2e^-$) quotients for respiration between various reductants and oxidants, both physiological and artificial, of different redox potential; when carried out in the presence of appropriate electron transfer inhibitors to prevent endogenous respiration, these experiments ensured that the respiratory chain was effectively dissected into discrete, functional segments. The results have repeatedly shown that the three phosphorylation sites (1, 2 and 3) are present in respiratory chain complexes I, III and IV, respectively (Fig. 4.1; Table 4.1); the alternative, external NADH dehydrogenase cytochrome-independent respiratory pathways in plant mitochondria, lack phosphorylation sites 1 and 2 + 3, respectively. A fourth site has recently been demonstrated at the level of transhydrogenase ($NADPH \rightarrow NAD^+$; site 0) by generating a high endogenous

Table 4.1 ATP/O ($ATP/2e^-$) quotients

Reductant	*Oxidant*	*Inhibitor*	*ATP/O(ATP/2e⁻)*
3-hydroxybutyrate (NADH)	O_2	—	3
Succinate	O_2	Rotenone	2
Ascorbate-ferrocyanide	O_2	Rotenone + antimycin A	1.5
3-hydroxybutyrate (NADH)	Ferricyanide	Cyanide	1.5
Succinate	Ferricyanide	Cyanide	0.5

[NADPH][NAD$^+$]:[NADP$^+$][NADH] ratio to produce a sufficiently large ΔE_h; however, since the required nucleotide concentrations are most unlikely to pertain *in vivo*, site 0 is probably of little significance to oxidative phosphorylation and it is principally associated with reversed electron transfer (Section 4.6). There is increasing evidence that each of the three energy coupling sites between NADH and oxygen exhibits a different *ATP/site ratio* (ATP/2e$^-$ quotient per site), viz. approximately 1, 0.5 and 1.5 at sites 1, 2 and 3, respectively; the non-unit values at sites 2 and 3 reflect the fact that the donors and acceptors react with the respiratory chain on different sides of the membrane (Section 5.2.1).

It should be noted that all of the above stoichiometries have been determined using exogenous ADP and phosphate. They therefore reflect the expenditure of redox energy not only for the synthesis of ATP but also for the transport of these reactants through the coupling membrane. The latter can theoretically be eliminated either by using submitochondrial particles or by measuring intramitochondrial oxidative phosphorylation. In practice, the former are often imperfectly coupled and hence do not exhibit maximal ATP/O quotients when measured kinetically (but see Section 5.2.3), but recent analyses of intramitochondrial respiration and ATP synthesis utilizing endogenous reactants have, interestingly, yielded significantly increased ATP/O quotients, i.e. the energy normally used for the translocation of adenine nucleotides and phosphate has been diverted to ATP synthesis.

The determination of accurate and quantitative ATP/O or ATP/2e$^-$ quotients in whole bacteria has met with limited success, mainly because the absence of an adenine nucleotide translocase necessitates the experimentally difficult task of measuring intracellular ATP formation net of any competing hydrolytic reactions. This problem can, of course, be circumvented by using inside-out membrane vesicles, but the latter are usually imperfectly sealed and hence are poorly coupled; ATP/O quotients for the oxidation of NAD$^+$-linked substrates rarely approach 3 with the latter technique. Nevertheless, by using appropriate reductants and oxidants it has been shown that the respiratory chains of aerobic bacteria, like mammalian mitochondria, contain up to four energy coupling sites; sites 1 and 2 appear to be everpresent (although site 1 can be deleted during iron- or sulphate-limited growth), whereas sites 0 and 3 depend upon the presence of energy-dependent transhydrogenase and cytochrome *c* respectively. Site 0 is usually involved in reversed electron transfer rather than ATP synthesis, as also are sites 1 and 2 during the oxidation of high redox potential reductants (e.g. hydroxylamine, nitrite and Fe^{2+}) by various species of chemolithotrophic bacteria. Similarly, the reduction of low redox potential oxidants (e.g. fumarate, nitrate and sulphite) during anaerobic respiration only allows ATP synthesis at sites 2 and/or 1. These conclusions are generally supported by measurements of *molar growth yields*, i.e. the amount of cell mass which is produced per mole of carbon source consumed, electron donor oxidized or electron acceptor reduced during energy-limited growth.

4.2 Respiratory control

In 1956 Chance and Williams reported that in the presence of non-limiting concentrations of reductant, oxygen and phosphate, the respiratory activity of intact mitochondria was effectively controlled by the availability of ADP; this phenomenon is called *respiratory control* [23]. In the absence of ADP, respiratory activity is low and reflects the slow rate of endogenous energy dissipation (*controlled state* or *state* 4; Fig. 4.2a). Following the addition of ADP, the rate of respiration increases dramatically and ultimately becomes limited by the activity of the chain or the ATP/ADP translocase (*active state* or *state* 3). The rate remains fast until the ADP is almost completely esterified, at which point it declines to the state 4 rate again. Successive ADP-induced cycles of this type can be observed until the reaction mixture becomes depleted of reductant, oxygen or phosphate. These results indicate that respiration and energy conservation are tightly coupled in intact mitochondria, the former being controlled by the requirement for the latter such that, under normal conditions, unnecessary respiration does not occur.

Two important parameters can be calculated from this type of experiment, viz. the *ADP/O quotient* (≡ P/O or ATP/O quotient) and the *respiratory control index* (RCI). Since the extent of state 3 respiration is determined by the amount of ADP available, the addition of 0.50 μmol ADP to state 4 mitochondria oxidizing succinate (Fig. 4.2a) causes the rapid uptake of an extra 0.245 μg-atom oxygen, and the ADP/O quotient is therefore 0.50/0.245 = 2.08 mol ADP·g-atom O^{-1}; the oxidation of NAD^+-linked substrates and ferrocyanide yields ADP/O quotients of approximately 3 and 1.5, respectively. The respiratory control index is simply the ratio of the state 3: state 4 respiration rates; its value, which

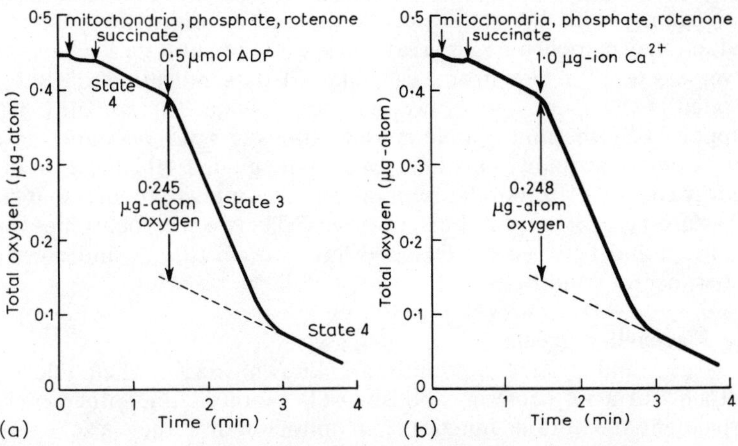

Fig. 4.2 The effect of (a) ADP, and (b) Ca^{2+} on mitochondrial respiration.

Table 4.2 Comparison of redox states

State	*Aerobic steady state (% reduction)*				
	NAD^+	Fp	*b(total)*	$c(+c_1)$	*a*
3	53	20	16	6	4
4	99	40	35	14	0

rarely exceeds 7, is a sensitive guide to the 'tightness' of energy coupling and hence to the integrity of the coupling membrane.

Apart from ATP synthesis, respiration can drive several other energy-dependent membrane functions, including ion transport (Section 3.3). Thus the addition of a small amount of Ca^{2+} to state 4 mitochondria oxidizing succinate (Fig. 4.2b) elicits a short-term increase in respiratory activity which lasts until virtually all of the Ca^{2+} has been imported; quantitatively, 1.0 μg-ion Ca^{2+} causes the uptake of an extra 0.248 μg-atom O to yield a Ca^{2+}/O quotient of 4.03 g-ion Ca^{2+}·g-atom 0^{-1}. The oxidation of NAD^+-linked substrates and ferrocyanide yields Ca^{2+}/O quotients of approximately 6 and 3, respectively, i.e. the transport of two Ca^{2+} is energetically equivalent to the synthesis of one molecule of ATP.

Respiratory control has only rarely been demonstrated in bacteria. In whole cells this probably reflects the high activities *in vitro* of various energy-dissipating processes (e.g. ion transport and ATP-hydrolysing metabolic reactions), whereas the absence of tight coupling is probably the major reason with inside-out membrane vesicles.

4.3 Crossover points

Dual wavelength spectrophotometry of respiring mitochondria indicates that the aerobic steady state reduction levels of the redox carriers vary significantly with the respiratory state. For example, the percentage reduction of cytochrome *a* is greater in state 3 than in state 4, whereas the reverse is true for cytochrome *c* (Table 4.2), thus indicating that site 3 is located in the span $c \rightarrow a$. However, since this conclusion is only partly supported by thermodynamic considerations, a state 3 → state 4 crossover point is probably only an approximate guide to the location of an energy coupling site. Similar reservations also apply to reports that state 3 → state 4 crossover points can be observed between cytochromes *b* and *c* (site 2) and between NADH and flavoprotein (site 1) under certain experimental conditions.

4.4 Uncoupling agents

A large number of compounds are known which, when added to mitochondria or bacteria, abolish ATP synthesis and other energy-dependent membrane functions; in mitochondria they also cause a several-fold stimulation of respiration. These compounds are called

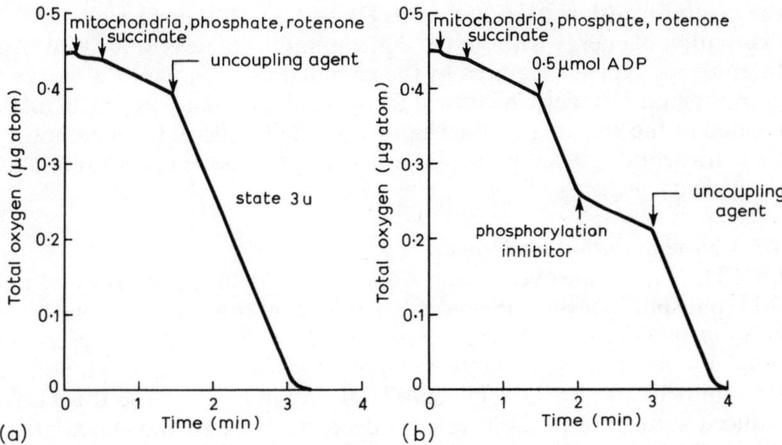

Fig. 4.3 The effect of (a) an uncoupling agent and (b) a phosphorylation inhibitor on mitochondrial respiration.

uncoupling agents, and the mitochondria are said to be in the *uncoupled state* or *state* 3*u* (Fig. 4.3a). The majority of uncoupling agents are lipophilic weak acids such as 2,4-dinitrophenol (DNP) and carbonyl cyanide *p*-trifluoromethoxyphenylhydrazone (FCCP; Fig. 4.4); uncoupling can also be effected in the presence of K^+ by a mixture of the K^+-ionophores valinomycin and nigericin, neither of which will uncouple alone, and by physical disruption of the coupling membrane using detergents or ultrasound. Uncoupling agents appear to affect each energy coupling site to a similar degree, and are independent of ADP and phosphate. It is likely, therefore, that respiration is coupled to energy conservation via a non-phosphorylated, energized state which is dissipated by membrane-active protonophores (e.g. lipophilic anions, valinomycin + nigericin + K^+) and by non-specific membrane-disrupting agents. There is some evidence that lipophilic anions combine tightly with the uncoupler-binding protein located on the M-side of F_0 in the ATP phosphohydrolase complex, but whether such binding is essential to their mechanism of action remains to be elucidated [24].

Interestingly, mitochondria from thermogenic brown adipose tissue are naturally uncoupled [25]. Nicholls has shown that they contain an active H^+-uniport in their coupling membrane, which is distinct from

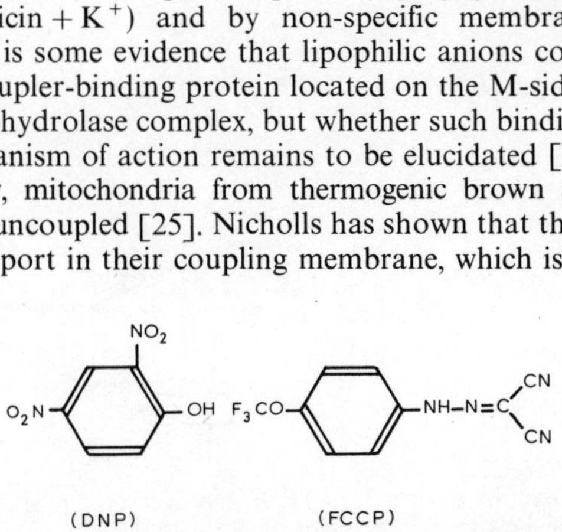

NO_2 — O_2N — OH — F_3CO — NH–N=C(CN)(CN)

(DNP) (FCCP)

Fig. 4.4 The structures of DNP and FCCP.

the proton-translocating channel in F_0, and which therefore allows the dissipation of energy without the concomitant synthesis of ATP. When thermogenesis is not required by the animal, this H^+-uniport is blocked by purine nucleotides which bind to a specific protein (mol. wt. 32 000) located at the entrance to the channel on the C-side of the membrane; these nucleotides therefore act in brown adipose tissue mitochondria as *recoupling agents*.

4.5 Phosphorylation inhibitors

DCCD, Nbf-Cl, aurovertin and oligomycin inhibit the activity of the ATP phosphohydrolase (Section 3.2) and hence are classed as *phosphorylation inhibitors*; carboxyatractyloside may be similarly described since, by blocking ATP/ADP transport it inhibits phosphorylation of extramitochondrial ADP. Phosphorylation inhibitors cause the ADP-induced state 3 respiration rate to decrease back to the state 4 rate (Fig. 4.3b), but they have no affect on the state 3 rate induced by Ca^{2+} or uncoupling agents. Importantly, however, the addition of an uncoupling agent to mitochondria already affected by a phosphorylation inhibitor completely restores the state 3 rate, but uncoupler-stimulated ATPase activity is strongly depressed by phosphorylation inhibitors. These observations have important implications for the mechanism of oxidative phosphorylation since they indicate that uncoupling agents act closer than phosphorylation inhibitors to the primary energized state generated by respiration.

4.6 Reversed electron transfer

Since respiration and ATP synthesis are tightly coupled, the exergonic nature of ATP hydrolysis should allow it to drive respiration in reverse (*ATP-dependent reversed electron transfer*). This hypothesis was independently proved in 1960 by Chance and Klingenberg, who de-

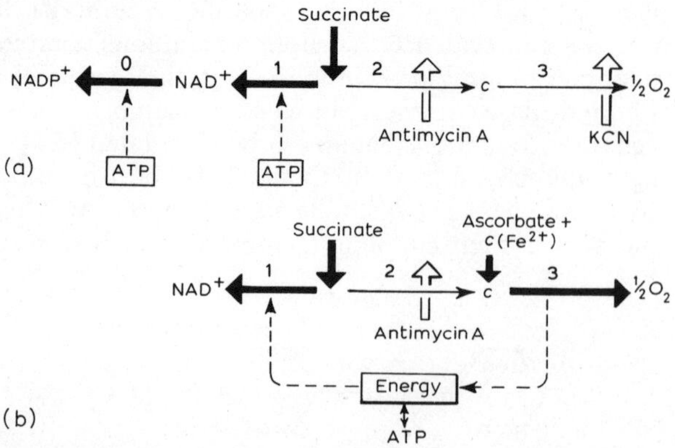

Fig. 4.5 Reversed electron transfer. (a) ATP-dependent reversal of sites 1 and 0, and (b) aerobic reversal of site 1 at the expense of site 3.

monstrated that intact mitochondria catalyse the reduction of NAD^+ by succinate at the expense of ATP (reversal of site 1; Fig. 4.5a); later experiments readily demonstrated the ATP-dependent reversal of sites 0($NADP^+ \leftarrow NADH$) and 1+2 ($NAD^+ \leftarrow$ascorbate-ferrocytochrome *c*), but the reversal of site 3 (ferricytochrome $c \leftarrow H_2O$) was only achieved with difficulty. These reactions proceed optimally under anaerobic conditions, or when the respiratory chain is blocked by the addition of appropriate inhibitors. The ATP-dependent reversal of site 1 has been investigated in some detail; it is highly efficient energetically, exhibiting an ATP hydrolysed/site ratio of approximately 2 in mitochondria and 1.3 in submitochondrial particles. This difference in stoichiometry is interesting and, once again, probably reflects the expenditure of energy for adenine nucleotide transport in the former but not the latter.

Reversed electron transfer at sites 0, 1 and 2 can also occur at the expense of energy conserved during forward electron transfer at sites 1, 2 or 3 (*aerobic reversed electron transfer*; Fig. 4.5b). This phenomenon is inhibited by uncoupling agents but, unlike ATP-dependent reversal, is unaffected or even slightly stimulated by phosphorylation inhibitors.

Reversed electron transfer in mitochondria is probably of limited importance physiologically, although the ability to generate NADPH at the expense of NADH may be of significance to biosynthesis. In contrast, the ability of many species of chemolithotrophic bacteria to reduce $NAD(P)^+$ at the expense of higher redox potential, inorganic reductants is absolutely crucial to their autotrophic mode of life (Section 2.8). However, the energy expenditure on reversed electron transfer in an organism such as *Nitrobacter*, which has to oxidize at least two molecules of nitrite via site 3 in order to drive a pair of electrons backwards from a third molecule to NAD^+ over sites 2 and 1, is enormous and is reflected in the very low molar growth yield of this chemolithotroph; growth of other organisms on NH_2OH or Fe^{2+} is similarly affected.

4.7 The energized state

There is now convincing evidence that the transfer of energy between the respiratory chain, the ATP phosphohydrolase and the various solute transport systems is both efficient and fully reversible, and that it occurs via a common and stable, non-phosphorylated energized state (Fig. 4.6). The latter is dissipated by protonophoric uncoupling agents, but not by phosphorylation inhibitors. Thus respiration will drive ATP synthesis, ATP hydrolysis will drive reversed electron transfer, and both respiration and ATP hydrolysis will drive solute transport; similarly, certain solute gradients of the correct magnitude and direction will power both ATP synthesis and reversed electron transfer. The ability to use ATP hydrolysis and solute export for membrane energization is of particular importance to fermentative bacteria, which conserve energy

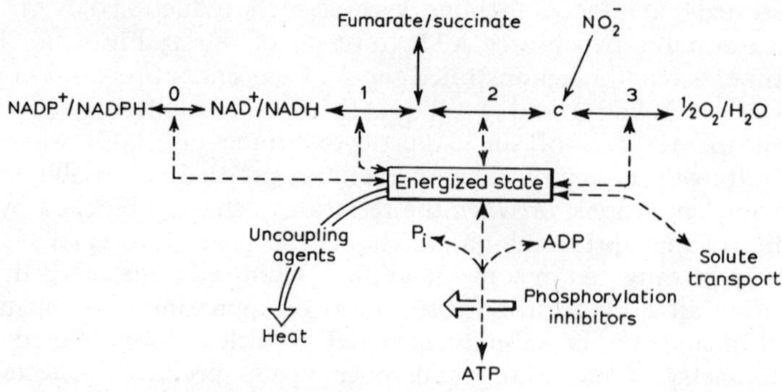

Fig. 4.6 The membrane energized state.

solely via substrate level phosphorylation. It is clear; therefore, that the energized state occupies a central position in the mechanism of membrane-associated energy transduction.

5 Mechanisms of oxidative phosphorylation

The unambiguous identification of the primary energized state remains the major problem of contemporary bioenergetics. During the last thirty years, four major hypotheses have been put forward to describe the mechanism of oxidative phosphorylation and related membrane processes, viz. the *chemical*, *chemiosmotic*, *localised proton* and *conformational* hypotheses [26].

5.1 The chemical hypothesis

The chemical hypothesis, which was first proposed by Slater in 1953 [27], is based upon substrate-level phosphorylation in which oxidation–reduction leads to ATP synthesis via the sequential, stoichiometric formation of non-phosphorylated and phosphorylated covalent intermediates (Section 1.4). The essential features of this hypothesis may be summarized as follows:

$$\begin{aligned}
AH_2 + B + I{\cdot}OH &\rightleftharpoons A \sim I + BH_2 + OH^- \\
A \sim I + X{\cdot}H &\rightleftharpoons X \sim I + A + H^+ \\
X \sim I + P{\cdot}OH &\rightleftharpoons X \sim P + I{\cdot}OH \\
X \sim P + ADP &\rightleftharpoons ATP + X{\cdot}H \\
\hline
AH_2 + B + ADP + P\,OH &\rightleftharpoons A + BH_2 + ATP + H_2O
\end{aligned}$$

AH_2 and B are the respiratory carriers which span the energy coupling site, and are capable of forming anhydride bonds with high free energies of hydrolysis. Alternative formulations envisage the initial formation of $BH_2 \sim I$ instead of $A \sim I$, and the cleavage of $X \sim I$ by ADP and phosphate without the intermediate formation of $X \sim P$.

Classically, verification of this hypothesis requires that the intermediates be identified and isolated. This may be unreasonable in the case of $X \sim I$ since the latter need be present only in very low concentrations and may be unstable outside the hydrophobic milieu of the coupling membrane; in contrast, $A \sim I$ (or $BH_2 \sim I$) involves a respiratory chain carrier and should at least be detectable by absorption or EPR spectroscopy. Several candidates have been proposed, but all have been found wanting when subjected to close scrutiny. The chemical hypothesis is now generally regarded as being untenable.

5.2 The chemiosmotic hypothesis

The suggestion that the mechanism of oxidative phosphorylation involves protons was first made independently by Mitchell and Williams in 1961. It was subsequently expanded by Mitchell, in collaboration with Jennifer Moyle, into the elegant and persuasive chemiosmotic hypothesis [28, 29]. The latter is so called since it is postulated to involve chemical reactions (the transfer of e^-, H and O^{2-} within the membrane) and an osmotic reaction (the transport of a solute, H^+, across the membrane). The essential tenets of chemiosmosis are, therefore, that oxidative phosphorylation requires (i) an *anisotropic* (direction-oriented) proton-translocating respiratory chain, (ii) a coupling membrane which is impermeable to ions except via specific exchange-diffusion systems, and (iii) an anisotropic proton-translocating ATP phosphohydrolase. Thus, protons ejected via respiration generate a delocalized (transmembrane) protonmotive force (Δp, internal compartment alkaline and electrically negative; Section 3.3), which in turn drives ATP synthesis via the re-entry of protons through the ATP phosphohydrolase. Energy transduction is therefore mediated via a proton current (*proticity*), which circulates through the insulating membrane and the surrounding bulk aqueous phases (Fig. 5.1a); since the latter are in full equilibrium, energy storage is transmembranous rather than intramembranous.

5.2.1 *The proton-translocating respiratory chain*

The view that mitochondria and bacteria contain an outwardly-directed, proton-translocating respiratory chain is based upon the observation that when a small quantity of dissolved oxygen or an alternative electron acceptor is added to a lightly buffered anaerobic suspension, the surrounding medium undergoes a rapid acidification followed by a slow re-alkalinization as the ejected protons re-equilibrate across the coupling membrane (Fig. 5.1b); the direction of proton movement is reversed in submitochondrial particles and inside-out bacterial vesicles. Since the coupling membrane has a very low electrical

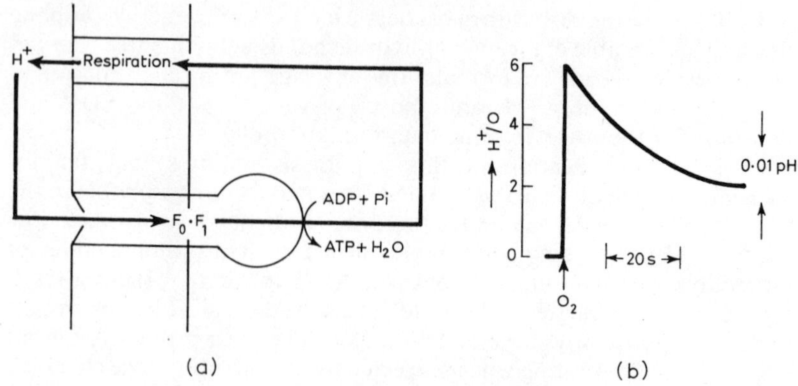

Fig. 5.1 (a) The chemiosmotic proton current, and (b) the measurement of $\rightarrow H^+/O$ quotients by the oxygen pulse procedure (after Mitchell and Moyle, 1967).

capacitance, maximum acidification is observed only when the membrane potential component of the protonmotive force ($\Delta\psi$) is collapsed by the concomitant movement of other ions, e.g. by the entry of cations such as Ca^{2+} or K^+ (via the Ca^{2+} carrier or added valinomycin, respectively) or by the outward diffusion of a permeant anion such as SCN^- (following preincubation in the presence of KSCN).

Respiration may therefore be written as:

$$DH_2 + A + zH^+_{(in)} \rightleftharpoons zH^+_{out} + D + AH_2$$

where DH_2 is the donor, A is the acceptor and z is numerically equal to the $\rightarrow H^+/O(\rightarrow H^+/2e^-)$ *quotient* or $\rightarrow$*acid/O quotient* (g-ion $H^+ \cdot$g-atom O^{-1}) the value of which is determined by the identity of the donor and acceptor, and by the composition and organization of the redox carriers in the respiratory chain. Mitchell and many other workers have reported $\rightarrow H^+/O$ quotients of approximately 8, 6 and 4 for the mitochondrial oxidation of exogenous substrates via internal $NADP^+$, NAD^+ and flavin, respectively. Similar results have been obtained with several species of bacteria (e.g. *Pc. denitrificans, Alc. eutrophus*) but those organisms which lack cytochrome *c* and show little or no energy-linked transhydrogenase activity (e.g. *E. coli*) exhibit maximum $\rightarrow H^+/O$ quotients of approximately 4. In addition, $\rightarrow H^+/O$ quotients in the range 0–6 have been observed during the aerobic oxidation of various inorganic reductants by chemolithotrophic bacteria, and $\rightarrow H^+/2e^-$ quotients approaching 2 and 4 have been reported for the anaerobic oxidation of NADH by fumarate and nitrate, respectively. It has been concluded, therefore, that each respiratory chain energy coupling site ejects protons with an $\rightarrow$*H*$^+$*/site ratio* of 2. Each site was originally envisaged as a transmembrane *redox loop* consisting of a hydrogen carrier (e.g. flavin, Q) followed by an electron carrier (e.g. FeS, cytochrome); the ejection of $2H^+$ at each loop would thus occur via the outward transfer of 2H, followed by the inward transfer of $2e^-$

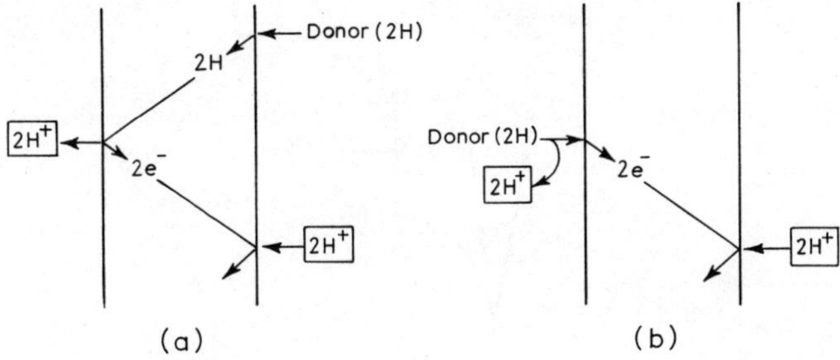

Fig. 5.2 Proton translocation via (a) a redox loop, and (b) a redox arm.

(Fig. 5.2a). However, only an electron-transferring *redox arm* would need to be present if the hydrogen donor reacts at the outside surface of the membrane (as during the oxidation of H_2 via hydrogenase in *E. coli*; Fig. 5.2b). The redox carrier composition at sites 1 and 2 is compatible with a redox loop mechanism, and proton ejection during the reduction of oxygen or nitrate by *E. coli* and similar organisms may well occur in this way (Fig. 5.3a). However, transhydrogenase contains no detectable redox carriers (which means that a completely different mechanism for proton translocation must operate at site 0) and cytochrome oxidase lacks a suitable hydrogen carrier. The latter problem is solved if sites 2 and 3 are fused into a complicated *protonmotive quinone cycle* [8, 29]

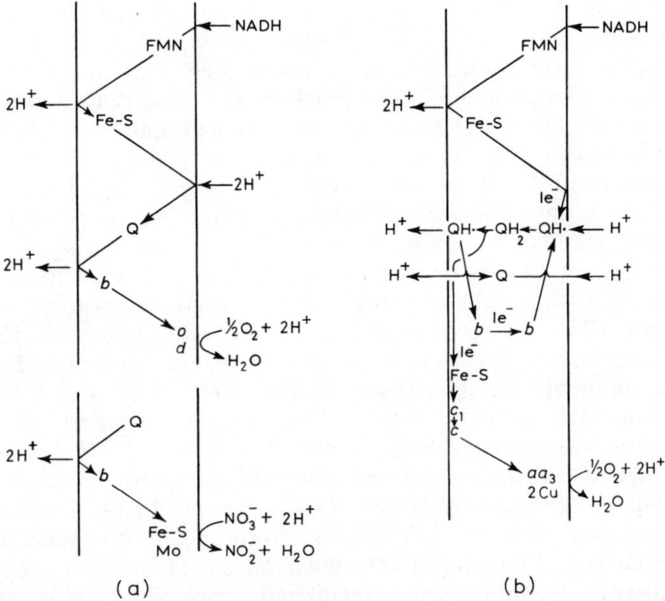

Fig. 5.3 Proton-translocating respiratory chains. (a) *E. coli*, and (b) mitochondria and some bacteria.

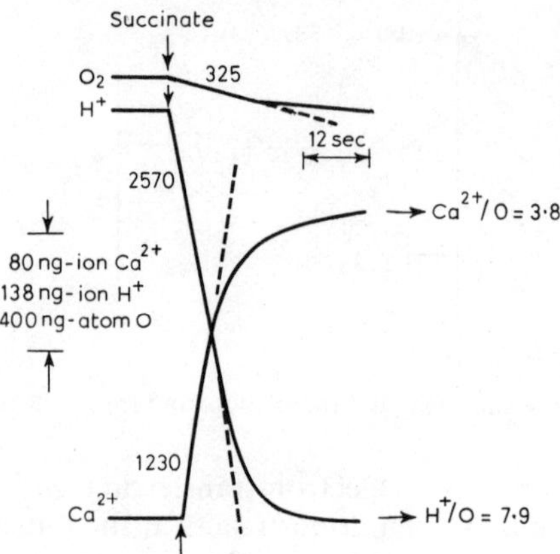

Fig. 5.4 The measurement of $\rightarrow H^+/O$ and $\rightarrow$charge/O quotients by the initial rate procedure (after Lehninger, 1979).

which involves the quinone, semiquinone and quinol forms of a single hydrogen carrier (Q or MK) and which catalyses the ejection of $4H^+$ ($2 \times 2H^+$) during two successive one-electron transfers from an iron–sulphur centre in the primary dehydrogenase to cytochrome *c*; cytochrome oxidase would, therefore, function simply as a vectorial electron carrier (Fig. 5.3b). These concepts are compatible with an $\rightarrow H^+/O$ quotient of 0 for the oxidation of ferrocyanide via cytochrome *c*, and with the intramembrane locations of the respiratory chain components.

However, recent work in several laboratories, particularly those of Lehninger, Azzone and Wikström, has raised some doubts about the values of mitochondrial $\rightarrow H^+/O$ quotients determined from oxygen-pulse experiments [30]. These workers claim that proton ejection may be underestimated owing to the rapid, ΔpH-dependent uptake of weak acids, such as phosphate, which leak out of the mitochondria during the anaerobic incubation phase. Thus, when phosphate transport is inhibited (e.g. by NEM) or eliminated (e.g. following depletion of the phosphate pool by anaerobic washing), the $\rightarrow H^+/O$ quotients for the oxidation of NAD^+-linked substrates and succinate increase to at least 9 and 6 respectively. These experiments have been criticised by Mitchell, who additionally has reported that the $\rightarrow H^+/O$ quotients for the oxidation of artificial substrates via cytochrome *c* are unaffected by these treatments; the latter have no effect on bacterial $\rightarrow H^+/O$ quotients.

A different method for determining $\rightarrow H^+/O$ quotients is currently receiving considerable attention. Developed by Lehninger and his colleagues, it entails measuring the initial rates of proton ejection and oxygen consumption which follow the addition of oxidizable substrates to lightly-buffered mitochondria incubated aerobically in the presence of Ca^{2+}, or valinomycin plus K^+ (Fig. 5.4). In the presence of low concentrations of NEM, $\rightarrow H^+/O$ quotients of up to 12, 8 and 4 have

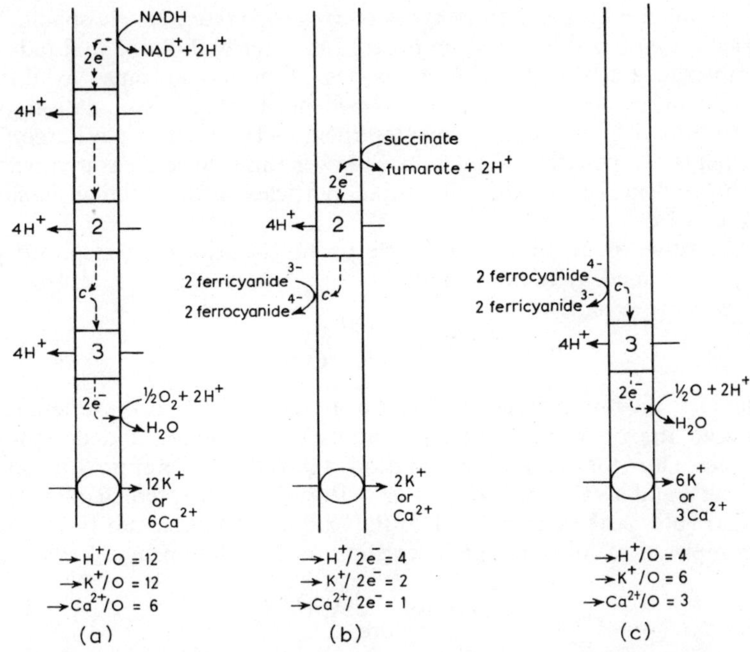

Fig. 5.5 Proton and charge movements during respiration at (a) sites 1, 2 and 3, (b) site 2, and (c) site 3.

been obtained for the oxidation of NAD^+-linked substrates, succinate and ferrocyanide respectively. That these values represent the true stoichiometries can be seen from the simultaneous measurement of $\rightarrow$*charge*/O *quotients* (i.e. $\rightarrow Ca^{2+}/O$ or $\rightarrow K^+/O$ quotients) which, unlike the measured $\rightarrow H^+/O$ quotients, are unaffected by the subsequent entry of phosphate or other weak acids. $\rightarrow$Charge/O quotients of approximately 8 and 6 have been reported for the oxidation of succinate and ferrocyanide, respectively, and $\rightarrow$charge/$2e^-$ quotients of approximately 6 and 2 characterize the oxidation of NADH and succinate by ferricyanide. Thus although sites 1, 2 and 3 each exhibit a maximum $\rightarrow H^+$/site ratio of 4, their *charge/site ratios* are 4, 2 and 6, respectively. These apparent discrepancies are simply explained by the fact that ferrocyanide and ferricyanide donate and accept electrons on the C-side of the membrane; the reduction of ferricyanide thus leads to the net loss of two charges, and the oxidation of ferrocyanide leads to the net gain of the same amount (Fig.5.5). This high $\rightarrow H^+$/site ratio is not commensurate with a simple redox loop mechanism of proton translocation, although it could be accommodated at site 2 by a protonmotive quinone cycle, and at the other sites by *membrane Bohr effects* (proton *pumps*; see Section 5.4) possibly supplemented by redox loops.

The ability of transhydrogenase and respiratory chain complexes I, III and IV to catalyse respiration-linked proton translocation has recently been confirmed using various types of *proteoliposomes*, i.e. phospholipid vesicles (*liposomes*) inlaid in an ordered manner with individual redox complexes. Each of these four species of proteoliposomes exhibits significant respiratory control, as evidenced by the stimulation of respiration by uncoupling agents; their $\rightarrow H^+/O$ and $\rightarrow$charge/O quotients are generally similar to or lower than those measured with mitochondria or submitochondrial particles using similar assay procedures.

The value of Δp generated by the proton-translocating respiratory chain is defined by the equation:

$$\Delta p = \frac{n \cdot \Delta E_h}{\rightarrow H^+/O} \tag{5.1}$$

where n is the number of electrons transferred, and ΔE_h is the difference between the operating redox potentials of the donor and acceptor couples. Thus, for the aerobic oxidation of NADH, ΔE_h is approximately 1140 mV and a value of $2 \times 1140/12 = 190$ mV can be predicted for Δp; similar values can be calculated for the oxidation of other substrates. Δp is comprised of $\Delta\psi$ and ΔpH according to the relationship:

$$\Delta p = \Delta\psi - z \cdot \Delta \text{pH} \tag{5.2}$$

where $z = 2.303\,RT/F$ ($\equiv 60$ at 25°C) and serves to convert ΔpH into electrical units (mV). Experimental determinations of Δp via the separate measurement of $\Delta\psi$ and ΔpH (Section 3.5), have yielded an average value of approximately 180 mV for state 4 respiration, and a slightly lower value for state 3. Since these values are slightly lower than predicted, it is possible either that the $\rightarrow H^+/O$ quotients are inaccurate or that the estimation of Δp between the bulk aqueous phases is not a reliable guide to the true thermodynamic potential of the energized state. Values of Δp in the range 100 – 230 mV have been obtained with several species of intact bacteria, and with sphaeroplasts and both types of membrane vesicles derived from them; at present it is not possible to say whether this variation reflects differences in structural integrity, respiratory chain composition (and hence ΔE_h) and/or methods of analysis.

5.2.2 *The ion-impermeable coupling membrane; exchange-diffusion*

Since the function of the proton-translocating respiratory chain is to develop a Δp of sufficient magnitude to drive ATP synthesis (and other energy-dependent functions) it is essential that the coupling membrane should be (i) topologically closed and (ii) virtually impermeable to ions, particularly H^+ and OH^-, except via specific exchange-diffusion systems. These requirements have been confirmed experimentally; the functional coupling membrane of mitochondria and bacteria is in-

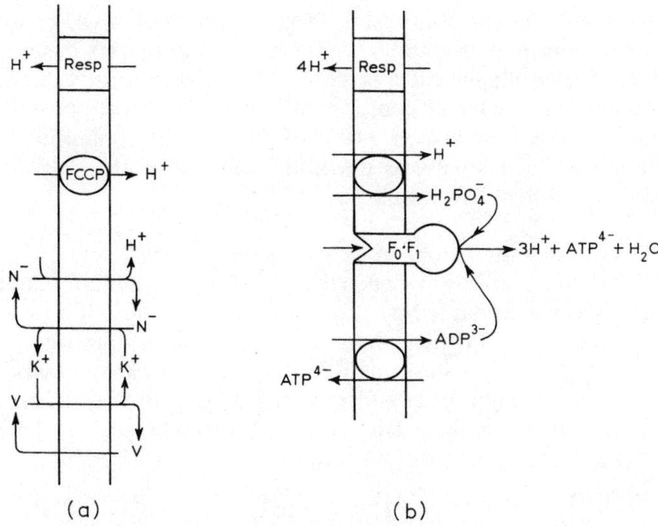

Fig. 5.6 (a) Uncoupling by FCCP and nigericin + valinomycin + K^+, and (b) ion movements during steady state oxidative-phosphorylation.

variably vesicular, and its effective proton conductance (CmH^+) is approximately one million times less than that of the surrounding aqueous phases (i.e. $\leq 0.5\,\mu$mho cm^{-2} or 0.2 nmol H^+ min^{-1} mg^{-1} mVΔp^{-1}).

Since $\Delta p \propto 1/CmH^+$ and, according to chemiosmosis, the back pressure of the Δp controls the rate of respiration, the latter is effectively determined by CmH^+. In state 4 mitochondria, the inward flow of protons via the ATP phosphohydrolase is restricted by the lack of ADP, and the activity of the proton-translocating respiratory chain is thus held severely in check by the resultant high Δp; the redox and energy transduction systems approach equilibrium. The addition of ADP, in the presence of phosphate, stimulates proton re-entry via the ATP phosphohydrolase, thus decreasing Δp by 10–30 mV and so allowing the rate of respiration to increase (state 3). A similar increase in respiratory activity is also effected when the proton conductance of the membrane is increased by the addition of uncoupling agents (state 3u), although on these occasions the required decrease in Δp is very much larger and may even be total. This discrepancy adds further weight to the possibility that the inter-bulk phase Δp may imperfectly reflect the actual driving force for energy conservation.

In order to effect uncoupling, both the $\Delta\psi$ and ΔpH components of Δp must be collapsed. Reagents which collapse only ΔpH (e.g. nigericin + K^+) or $\Delta\psi$ (e.g. Ca^{2+}, or valinomycin + K^+), cause a transient stimulation of respiratory activity which leads to a compensatory increase in $\Delta\psi$ or ΔpH, respectively, such that uncoupling does not occur (Fig. 5.6a).

The presence in mitochondrial and bacterial coupling membranes of tightly coupled, exchange-diffusion systems which catalyse cation·H^+ antiport and anion H^+ symport (≡ anion·OH^- antiport), ensures that respiration does not generate a large, and hence osmotically disruptive, ΔpH; $\Delta\psi$ is by far the larger component of Δp under most physiological conditions. These systems, in association with cation uniports, also allow the controlled transport of essential metabolites into and out of the internal compartment (Sections 3.3 and 3.5).

5.2.3 *The proton-translocating ATP phosphohydrolase*

There is now considerable evidence that ATP synthesis in mitochondria and bacteria is accompanied by proton re-entry via the ATP phosphohydrolase, and that ATP hydrolysis is characterized by proton ejection; the direction of proton movement during these two processes is, of course, reversed in submitochondrial particles and inside-out bacterial vesicles (and also in $BF_0 \cdot BF_1$ proteoliposomes). ATP synthesis/hydrolysis may, therefore, be written as:

$$ADP^{3-} + H_2PO_4^- + xH^+_{(out)} \rightleftharpoons xH^+_{(in)} + ATP^{4-} + H_2O$$

where phosphate is shown as consisting entirely of $H_2PO_4^-$ (cf. Equation 1.1) in order to avoid the complications of scalar ionization protons in addition to vectorial protons, and x is numerically equal to the *→H⁺/ATP quotient* (or *→H⁺/P quotient*; g-ion H^+·mol ATP^{-1}).

Direct measurements of the →H^+/ATP quotient during the anaerobic hydrolysis of small pulses of ATP by mitochondria, submitochondrial particles and $BF_0 \cdot BF_1$ proteoliposomes, have indicated values close to 2. However, since it is possible that proton leakage may not have been completely eliminated in mitochondria and submitochondrial particles, their observed →H^+/ATP quotient of 2 may have been underestimated; in contrast, the very high phospholipid:protein ratio in these particular proteoliposomes makes them essentially proton-impermeable. No →charge/ATP quotients have been reported.

The →H^+/ATP quotient has also been determined indirectly via the simultaneous measurement of Δp and the *phosphate* (*phosphorylation*) *potential*. In state 4, respiration and ATP synthesis/hydrolysis are in thermodynamic equilibrium; the work done by the redox system (ΔG_{ox}) is, therefore, matched by the back pressure of the phosphate potential (ΔG_p), where the latter is defined by the equation:

$$\Delta G_p = \Delta G^{\ominus\prime} + 2.303\,RT \log \frac{[ATP]}{[ADP][Pi]} \qquad (5.3)$$

in which $\Delta G^{\ominus\prime}$ is the standard free energy change of ATP hydrolysis. Since, according to chemiosmosis, this equilibrium is mediated via the bulk-phase Δp, then:

$$\Delta G_p = \rightarrow H^+/ATP \cdot \Delta p \qquad (5.4)$$

where ΔG_p is in V (kJ mol^{-1}/F). The average value for the extramitochondrial phosphate potential (ΔG_{pout}) is approximately 650 mV, which therefore yields an $\rightarrow H^+/ATP$ quotient of 650/180 = 3.6. In contrast, the average intramitochondrial value (ΔG_{pin}) is approximately 525 mV, which indicates an $\rightarrow H^+/ATP$ quotient of 2.9; similar values to these have been reported for submitochondrial particles. These results, therefore, indicate that the $\rightarrow H^+/ATP$ quotient of the ATP phosphohydrolase is close to 3, whereas the value for the overall synthesis or hydrolysis of ATP (i.e. including its transport through the coupling membrane) is significantly higher than this.

The lower value obtained for the *catalytic* $\rightarrow H^+/ATP$ *quotient* compared with the *overall* $\rightarrow H^+/ATP$ *quotient* in mitochondria means (i) that the combined action of the electrogenic adenine nucleotide translocase and the electroneutral phosphate transporter should consume up to one proton per molecule of ATP synthesized and exported (thus decreasing the value of ΔG_{pin} to well below that of ΔG_{pout}), and hence (ii) that the $\rightarrow$ATP/O quotient for the oxidation of a given substrate should be lower when measured extramitochondrially than when assayed either intramitochondrially or in submitochondrial particles (since ATP/O = $\rightarrow H^+/O$ divided by the appropriate $\rightarrow H^+/ATP$). The first prediction is supported by the overall properties of steady-state oxidative phosphorylation (Fig. 5.6b), and by reports that the average energy requirement for adenine nucleotide transport is similar to $\Delta G_{\text{pout}} - \Delta G_{\text{pin}}$ (i.e. + 10.1 kJ mol^{-1} or 105 mV, cf. 125 mV). The second prediction is supported by kinetic (Section 4.1) and thermodynamic measurements; in the latter case, the simultaneous estimation of n, ΔE_h and ΔG_p under near equilibrium conditions indicates an $\rightarrow$ATP/O quotient of over 4 for the oxidation of NADH by submitochondrial particles.

The terms ΔG_{pout} and overall $\rightarrow H^+/ATP$ quotient do not pertain in bacteria since the latter lack an adenine nucleotide translocase. Whole cells and inside-out membrane vesicles of *Pc. denitrificans* exhibit a ΔG_p of approximately 550 mV (i.e. close to ΔG_{pin} for mitochondria) and a maximum Δp of 175 mV, which thus indicate an $\rightarrow H^+/ATP$ quotient of just over 3. No experiments of this type have been reported for other bacterial respiratory chains, but $\rightarrow H^+/ATP$ quotients of approximately 2 have been reported for some photosynthetic bacteria.

Current results suggest, therefore, that mitochondria exhibit maximum $\rightarrow H^+$/site ratios and catalytic $\rightarrow H^+/ATP$ quotients which approach 4 and 3, respectively [31]; allowing a proton for transport, these values are commensurate with the extramitochondrial $\rightarrow$ATP/O quotient of 3 for the oxidation of NAD^+-linked substrates. In contrast, there is little evidence that bacteria generally exhibit $\rightarrow H^+$/site ratios greater than 2, although claims to this effect have been made in some laboratories for *Pc. denitrificans*. Furthermore, although an $\rightarrow H^+/ATP$ quotient of 3 has been reported for this pseudo-mitochondrial organism, the sparse data currently available for other species of bacteria suggest values of approximately 2.

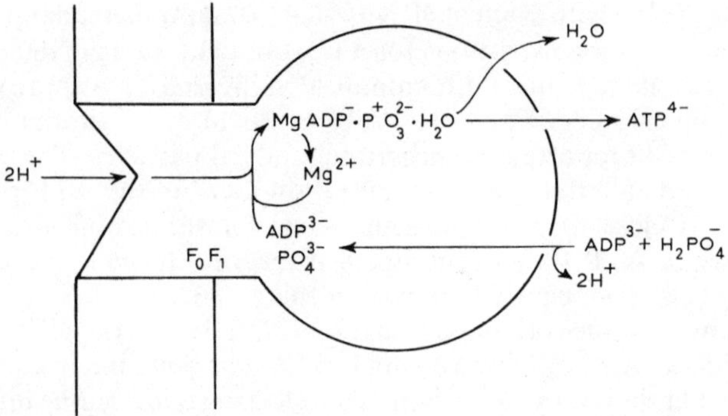

Fig. 5.7 A chemiosmotic mechanism of ATP synthesis.

It is now generally accepted that a Δp of the correct magnitude ($\nless 180\,\text{mV}$) and direction can displace the equilibrium of the mitochondrial or bacterial ATP phosphohydrolase reaction in the direction of ATP synthesis; indeed, artificially imposed gradients of ΔpH or $\Delta\psi$ alone can drive this reaction *in vitro*. The major problem, of course, lies in determining exactly how these delocalized forces drive the reaction. Several complicated and largely hypothetical schemes, based on a catalytic $\rightarrow H^+/ATP$ quotient of 2, have been proposed to describe the mechanism of ATP synthesis in chemiosmotic terms [29, 32]. A simplified version of one of these (Fig. 5.7) envisages that ADP^{3-} and phosphate reach the active site of F_1 via ligand conducting channels (e.g. basic arginyl or lysyl residues) which are specific to the required protonation/ionization-states of these reactants; during this process, protons are released into the internal compartment. The entry of protons from the external compartment occurs via an analogous type of conduction pathway through F_0, but which probably involves an ice channel or a chain of acid/base groups (e.g. histidyl residues); as a result of this proton movement, a bulk-phase Δp of 180 mV is entirely converted into a localized ΔpH of just over 3 units across the active site. O^{2-} is then transferred from phosphate to the incoming $2H^+$, whilst the resultant phosphorylium group ($P^+O_3^{2-}$) undergoes nucleophilic attack by $Mg\cdot ADP^-$ to form ATP^{4-}. The water and ATP^{4-} finally leave the active site via separate diffusion pathways through F_1. Similar schemes, involving different protonation states for ADP and phosphate, can be written to accommodate a catalytic $\rightarrow H^+/ATP$ quotient of 3. The driving force for the migration of the adenine nucleotides and phosphate into and out of the active site comes from their potential gradients, and the overall reaction is powered by Δp; ATP hydrolysis occurs via the reversal of this mechanism with the concomitant generation of Δp.

Chemiosmosis envisages that the transmembrane Δp generated by ATP hydrolysis or forward electron transfer (e.g. at site 3) is the driving force for reversed electron transfer (e.g. at site 1). The inward retranslocation of protons through complex I, and the resultant reduction of NAD^+ by succinate, thus occurs until Δp is matched by the backpressure of the redox reaction ($n{\cdot}\Delta E_h$ divided by $\rightarrow H^+/2e^-$).

5.3 The localized proton hypothesis

This hypothesis, which was developed by Williams [33], is not at variance with the central concept of chemiosmosis, viz. that ATP synthesis is driven by protons liberated during respiration. It differs fundamentally from chemiosmosis, however, in that it envisages the driving force as a localized (intramembrane or trans-interface) proton concentration, the diffusion of which is strictly controlled such that it does not rapidly equilibrate with the two adjacent aqueous phases; contact with these phases can occur however, at least *in vitro* but possibly only slowly, as evidenced by measurements of respiration- and ATP-linked proton translocation, and of ATP synthesis and ion-transport at the expense of artificially-imposed ΔpH and/or $\Delta\psi$. The concept of localized energy eliminates the osmotic element of chemiosmosis; thus, whereas the latter requires three phases, the localized proton hypothesis needs only two, viz. the membrane and the M-side aqueous phase (Fig. 5.8).

The initial energy-transducing event during respiration is viewed as being the separation of charge at a metal redox centre (e.g. Fe–S, cytochrome), to produce electrons and protons. After the latter have been used to drive ATP synthesis they return to the respiratory chain where, together with the electrons, they reduce either an organic redox centre (e.g. flavin, quinone) or the terminal oxidant. Since these steps may be accompanied by the localized release of Bohr protons (Section 5.4), they are perfectly compatible with an $\rightarrow H^+$/site ratio ≥ 2.

It is envisaged that the active site of the ATP phosphohydrolase contains several basic groups which readily bind ADP^{3-} and phosphate, and thus generate a significant, but currently unidentifiable, conformational change. The latter excludes water from the active site, but opens up a specific diffusion pathway, presumably in F_0, via which the

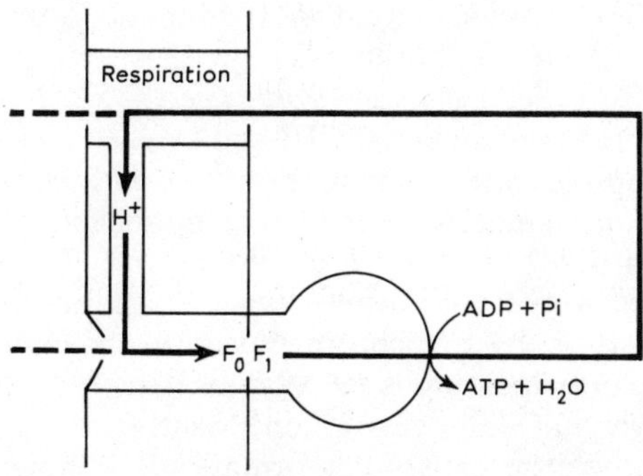

Fig. 5.8 Proton movements according to the localized proton hypothesis.

protons generated by the redox reactions can gain access (in the absence of ADP and phosphate, this channel is closed and respiration slows to the rate allowed by residual proton leakage; state 4). The resultant localized binding of $\geq 2H^+$ at the active site leads to further conformational changes which facilitate the removal of water from the locus of pyrophosphate condensation, thus driving the synthesis of ATP. On the release of ATP and water from F_1, the active site relaxes its conformation and is ready to receive another molecule each of ADP and phosphate. This mechanism of energy transduction can also accommodate both reversed electron transfer (via reversed proton flow from the active site to the first redox centre) and the action of uncoupling agents (which equilibrate the localized protons).

5.4 The conformational hypothesis

The conformational hypothesis, which was originally proposed by Boyer in 1965 and extensively modified thereafter, envisages that respiration generates protein conformational changes which are used to drive ATP synthesis. The transmission of these conformational changes between the redox and ATP synthesizing systems was originally thought to occur either by protein–protein interactions or via the formation of covalent intermediates, but more recent views favour protons [26, 34].

The use of fluorescent probes such as anilinonaphthalene sulphonate (ANS) and aurovertin, which bind to the membrane and exhibit enhanced or diminished fluorescence in response to changes in its conformation or hydrophobicity, has provided strong evidence that the redox complexes and the ATP phosphohydrolase can undergo conformational changes during respiration and oxidative phosphorylation. During respiration such changes can arise, for example, from small alterations in the Fe–N bond length in a particular cytochrome; these alterations are subsequently amplified by interactions between peptide chains such that the small movement of the central iron atom is translated into a significant change in the 'quaternary' structure of the redox complex. These structural modifications could lead to changes in the pK_a of appropriately located carboxyl or amino groups, and hence to the assymetric release and uptake of protons across or within the membrane (the so-called *membrane Bohr effect*) [35]. In this respect it is interesting to note that complexes I, III and IV each contain at least one hydrophobic peptide which might form a transmembrane or intramembrane proton channel similar to that present in F_0; indeed, liposomes inlaid with subunits 1 – 3 of cytochrome oxidase aa_3 exhibit greatly increased ion-translocating properties, and respiration-linked proton translocation by cytochrome oxidase proteoliposomes is inhibited by DCCD (which binds to subunit 3).

Recently, Boyer and Slater have independently provided evidence that membrane energization causes conformationally induced changes in substrate affinities at the active site of the ATP phosphohydrolase. They

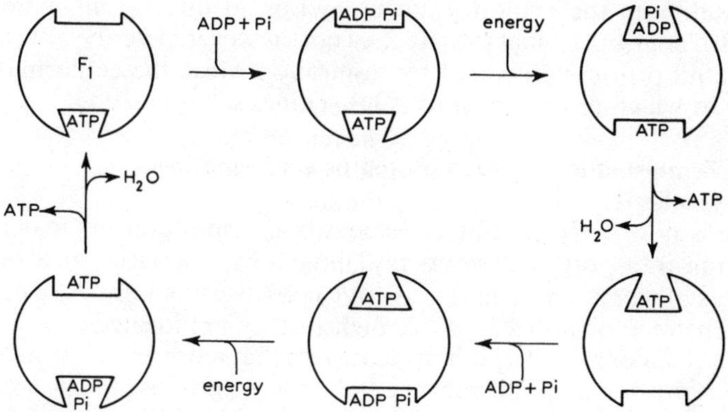

Fig. 5.9 The alternating catalytic site mechanism of ATP synthesis (after Boyer, 1977).

have suggested, therefore, that energy is not required to drive the condensation of ADP and phosphate *per se*, but rather to promote the binding of the reactants in a mode favourable to ATP synthesis, and to facilitate the release of synthesized ATP. This view stems mainly from observations that reactions which involve the release of bound ATP from the ATP phosphohydrolase are uncoupler-sensitive (e.g. ATP–phosphate exchange and ATP–water exchange), whereas those which do not require ATP release are insensitive (e.g. the hydrolysis of bound ATP and phosphate–water exchange). The further observations that (i) uncouplers increase the apparent K_m for ADP and phosphate, (ii) bound ATP is a rapidly formed intermediate in the net synthesis of ATP, and (iii) F_1 contains several adenine nucleotide-binding sites, including two catalytic sites and up to four regulatory sites (probably located on β and $\alpha\beta$ subunits, respectively), have led to the proposal that ATP synthesis occurs via an *alternating catalytic site mechanism* involving co-operative interactions between two catalytic domains (Fig. 5.9). This 'flip-flop' mechanism envisages that membrane energization causes conformational changes which promote the tight binding of ADP and phosphate at one catalytic site, whilst concomitantly loosening the binding of ATP at the other site; ATP is subsequently formed at the first site at the expense of the free energy of binding of the reactants (i.e. without further energy input), and ATP is released from the second site. The latter now binds ADP and phosphate, and the half-cycle essentially repeats itself to allow the release of ATP from the first site. The roles of the other four sites are currently unclear. It is interesting to note that a somewhat similar mechanism has been proposed for energy transduction at site 0; transhydrogenase, like the ATP phosphohydrolase, contains no redox carriers.

The conformational hypothesis adequately accounts for respiratory control and for reversed electron transfer at sites 1 and 2 by obvious interpretations of the above mechanism; uncoupling agents are thought to equilibrate the proton gradient and/or to directly dissipate constrained conformational sites. It does not, however, describe how the Δp or bound protons generated by respiration cause the conformational changes which are essential to ATP synthesis.

5.5 Chemiosmotic, localized proton or conformational hypothesis?

There is now fairly general agreement that respiration, ATP synthesis and ion-transport are reversibly linked by energized protons. In contrast, there is still remarkably little consensus on how these protons are generated or utilized, or even where they are located [36].

The chemiosmotic hypothesis envisages that redox loops, arms, cycles and/or proton pumps (membrane Bohr effects) give rise to a delocalized proton/charge gradient, the transmembrane Δp, which drives oxidative phosphorylation. However, both the general concept of field-driven chemical reactions and specific aspects of the proposed mechanism of ATP synthesis have been strongly criticised on theoretical grounds; it is also difficult to reconcile this mechanism with compelling evidence that energy is required for the binding and release of reactants rather than for pyrophosphate condensation *per se*. Chemiosmosis provides an appropriately vectorial mechanism for solute transport, an elegant rationale for the action of most uncoupling agents, and a simple but effective way of conserving energy by some types of bacterial respiratory chains (e.g. during the external oxidation of certain hydrogen donors). On the other hand, it has difficulty in adequately describing energy transduction in those species of bacteria which contain concentric layers of coupling membranes or which live in environments of extremely high pH (*alkaliphiles*).

These latter systems are more satisfactorily accommodated by the localized proton hypothesis which envisages that respiration generates intramembrane protons which bind to the active site of the ATP phosphohydrolase and, by withdrawing water, force the equilibrium of the reaction towards ATP synthesis. This mechanism, unlike chemiosmosis, invokes strict kinetic control (via conformational changes) on the diffusion of the reactants and products to and from the active site; it also emphasizes the role of water, and stresses the need for proton binding rather than proton transport. The postulated absence of osmosis implies that oxidative phosphorylation can occur in non-vesicular membranes, but this has yet to be confirmed experimentally. The localized proton hypothesis has also been criticised on the grounds that it is both mechanistically and stoichiometrically imprecise; the first criticism is perfectly valid and reflects current ignorance of the chemistry of the reactants at the active site of the ATP phosphohydrolase, but the second criticism is open to challenge. Indeed, Williams has repeatedly asserted that since oxidative phosphorylation involves the conversion of chemical energy into electrical energy and back again (substrate oxidation $\rightarrow$ charge separation $\rightarrow$ ATP), the current chemiosmotic preoccupation with measuring $\rightarrow H^+/O$, $\rightarrow H^+/ATP$ and Δp is an unnecessary over-elaboration of that hypothesis, and that the only obligatory stoichiometry is the ATP/O quotient. The undoubted existence of transmembrane proton/charge gradients *in vitro* (and possibly also *in vivo*) are viewed by the localized proton hypothesis simply as a means of storing excess energy.

The conformational hypothesis stresses the role in energy transduction of the conformational changes which undoubtedly accompany respiration and oxidative phosphorylation. Indeed, the concept that redox-induced conformational changes can elicit H^+ pumping is acceptable to the localized proton hypothesis and is becoming increasingly necessary to chemiosmosis. This concept has recently received added support from the observation that the chlorophyll-independent, photosynthetic bacterium *Halobacterium halobium* contains in its coupling membrane a purple protein, *bacteriorhodopsin*, which on illumination catalyses the asymmetric release and uptake of protons via specific conductance channels; this protein, like transhydrogenase and the ATP phosphohydrolase, contains no redox carriers. There is compelling enzymological evidence in favour of the alternating catalytic site mechanism of ATP synthesis, although the latter currently lacks a defined chemical mechanism and hence does not discriminate between the use of localized or delocalized energy.

It must be concluded, therefore, that none of these hypotheses currently affords a complete and experimentally acceptable description of respiratory chain energy transduction, although each may correctly define one or more aspects of this process. This compromise view has recently been advocated by Kell in his *electrodic model* of oxidative phosphorylation [37] (see also [38]), which envisages that the proton current is transmembrane, but that it is carried along localized channels on the surface of the membrane (i.e. in the Stern layer of high electrostatic potential) and only enters the bulk aqueous phases under conditions when $\Delta\psi$ is collapsed. More experimental work is clearly required, particularly to determine (i) whether localized or delocalized proton/charge gradients represent the primary energized state (e.g. by measuring the effect of pH buffers and chaotropic agents on energy transduction, by analysing intramembrane protonation states, and by comparing the kinetics of primary energization and ATP synthesis) and (ii) to elucidate the chemical pathway of oxidative phosphorylation.

Suggestions for further reading

A. General texts

Lehninger, A. L. (1975), *Biochemistry*, 2nd edition, Worth Publishers, New York.

Morris, J. G. (1974), *A Biologists Physical Chemistry*, 2nd edition, Edward Arnold, London.

Stanier, R. Y., Adelburg, E. A. and Ingraham, J. L. (1977), *General Microbiology*, 4th edition, Prentice Hall, New Jersey.

B. Specialized texts

Barrett, J. and Lemberg, R. (1973), *Cytochromes*, Academic Press, London.

Chappell, J. B. (1977), *ATP*, Carolina Biology Readers, Burlington

Gregory, R. P. F. (1974), *Biochemistry of Photosynthesis*, Wiley-Interscience.

Haddock, B. A. and Hamilton, W. A. eds. (1977), *Soc. Gen. Microbiol. Symp. 27: Microbial Energetics*, Cambridge University Press, Cambridge.

Hall, D. O. and Rao, K. K. (1977), *Photosynthesis* (*Studies in Biology* series, no. 37), 2nd edition, Edward Arnold, London.

Harrison, P. M. and Hoare, R. J. (1980), *Metals in Biochemistry* (Outline Studies Series). Chapman and Hall, London.

Jones, C. W. (1981), *Bacterial respiration and photosynthesis*, Thomas Nelson, London.

Keilin, D. (1966), *The history of cell respiration and cytochrome*, Cambridge University Press, Cambridge.

Krebs, H. A. and Kornberg, H. L. (1957), *Energy transformations in living matter*, Springer-Verlag, Heidelberg.

Racker, E. (1976), *A new look at mechanisms in bioenergetics*, Academic Press, New York.

Whittaker, P. A. (1978), *Mitochondria: structure, function and assembly*, Longman, London.

C. References

[1] Thauer, R. K., Jungermann, K. and Decker, K. (1977), *Bacterial Revs.* **41**, 100–180.

[2] Lipmann, F. (1941), *Adv. Enzymol.* **1**, 99–162.

[3] Krebs, H. A. (1979), *TIBS* **4**, 263–264.

[4] Rydström, J. (1977), *Biochim. Biophys. Acta* **463**, 155–184.

[5] Ragan, C. I. (1976), *Biochim. Biophys. Acta* **456**, 249–290.

[6] Onishi, T. (1979), *Membrane Proteins* **2**, 1–87.

[7] Hatefi, Y. and Stiggall, D. E. (1976), *The Enzymes* **13**, 175–197.

[8] Trumpower, B. and Katki, A. G. (1979), *Membrane proteins* **2**, 89–200.

[9] Capaldi, R. A. (1979), *Membrane proteins* **2**, 201–231.

[10] Hall, D. O., Rao, K. K. and Mullinger, R. (1975), *Biochem. Soc. Trans.* **3**, 470–479.

[11] Keilin, D. (1925), *Proc. Roy. Soc. London* **B98**, 312–339.

[12] Salemme, F. R. (1977), *Ann. Rev. Biochem.* **46**, 299–329.
[13] Malmström, B. G. (1979), *Biochim. Biophys. Acta* **549**, 281–303.
[14] Williams, R. J. P. (1973), *Biochem. Soc. Trans.* **1**, 1–27.
[15] Hogeboom, G. H., Schneider, W. C. and Pallade, G. E. (1947), *Proc. Soc. Exptl. Biol. Med.* **65**, 320–321.
[16] Fernandez-Moran, H., Oda, T., Blair, P. V. and Green, D. E. (1964), *J. Cell Biol.* **22**, 63–100.
[17] Harris, D. A. (1978), *Biochim. Biophys. Acta* **463**, 245–273.
[18] Penefsky, H. S. (1979), *Adv. Enzymol.* **49**, 223–280.
[19] DePierre, J. W. and Ernster, L. (1977), *Ann. Rev. Biochem.* **46**, 201–262.
[20] LaNoue, K. F. and Schoolwerth, A. C. (1979), *Ann. Rev. Biochem.* **48**, 871–922.
[21] Klingenberg, M. (1979), *TIBS*, **4**, 249–252.
[22] Nicholls, D. G. and Crompton, M. (1980), *FEBS. Letts.* **111**, 1–7.
[23] Chance, B. and Williams, G. R. (1956), *Adv. Enzymol.* **17**, 65–134.
[24] Hanstein, W. G. (1976), *TIBS* **1**, 65–67.
[25] Nicholls, D. G. (1979), *Biochim. Biophys. Acta* **549**, 1–29.
[26] Boyer, P. D., Chance, B., Ernster, L., Mitchell, P., Racker, E. and Slater, E. C. (1977), *Ann. Rev. Biochem.* **46**, 955–1026.
[27] Slater, E. C. (1953), *Nature* **172**, 975–978.
[28] Mitchell, P. (1966), *Biol. Revs.* **41**, 445–502.
[29] Mitchell, P. (1979), *Les Priz Nobel en 1978*, pp. 135–172, Nobel Foundation, Stockholm.
[30] Wikström, M. and Krab, K. (1979), *Biochim. Biophys. Acta* **549**, 177–222.
[31] Rottenberg, H. (1979), *Biochim. Biophys. Acta* **549**, 225–253.
[32] Mitchell, P. (1977), *FEBS Letts.* **78**, 1–20.
[33] Williams, R. J. P. (1978), *FEBS Letts.* **85**, 9–19.
[34] Boyer, P. D. (1977), *TIBS* **2**, 38–40.
[35] Papa, S. (1976), *Biochem. Biophys. Acta* **456**, 39–84.
[36] Fillingame, R. H. (1980), *Ann. Rev. Biochem.* **49**, 1079–1113.
[37] Kell, D. B. (1979), *Biochim. Biophys. Acta* **549**, 55–99.
[38] Archbold, G. P. R., Farrington, C. L., Mckay, A. M. and Malpress, F. H. (1976), *Biochem. Soc. Trans.* **4**, 91–94.

Index